Contents

Preface

To the general reader

Although the *Access to History* series has been designed with the needs of students studying the subject at higher examination levels very much in mind, it also has a great deal to offer the general reader. The main body of the text (i.e. ignoring the Study Guides at the ends of chapters) forms a readable and yet stimulating survey of a coherent topic as studied by historians. However, each author's aim has not merely been to provide a clear explanation of what happened in the past (to interest and inform): it has also been assumed that most readers wish to be stimulated into thinking further about the topic and to form opinions of their own about the significance of the events that are described and discussed (to be challenged). Thus, although no prior knowledge of the topic is expected on the reader's part, she or he is treated as an intelligent and thinking person throughout. The author tends to share ideas and possibilities with the reader, rather than passing on numbers of so-called 'historical truths'.

To the student reader

There are many ways in which the series can be used by students studying History at a higher level. It will, therefore, be worthwhile thinking about your own study strategy before you start your work on this book. Obviously, your strategy will vary depending on the aim you have in mind, and the time for study that is available to you.

If, for example, you want to acquire a general overview of the topic in the shortest possible time, the following approach will probably be the most effective:

1 Read Chapter 1 and think about its contents.
2 Read the 'Making notes' section at the end of Chapter 2 and decide whether it is necessary for you to read this chapter.
3 If it is, read the chapter, stopping at each heading to note down the main points that have been made.
4 Repeat stage 2 (and stage 3 where appropriate) for all the other chapters.

If, however, your aim is to gain a thorough grasp of the topic, taking however much time is necessary to do so, you may benefit from carrying out the same procedure with each chapter, as follows:

1 Read the chapter as fast as you can, and preferably at one sitting.
2 Study the flow diagram at the end of the chapter, ensuring that you understand the general 'shape' of what you have just read.

Preface

3 Read the 'Making notes' section (and the 'Answering essay questions' section, if there is one) and decide what further work you need to do on the chapter. In particularly important sections of the book, this will involve reading the chapter a second time and stopping at each heading to think about (and to write a summary of) what you have just read.
4 Attempt the 'Source-based questions' section. It will sometimes be sufficient to think through your answers, but additional understanding will often be gained by forcing yourself to write them down.

When you have finished the main chapters of the book, study the 'Further Reading' section and decide what additional reading (if any) you will do on the topic.

This book has been designed to help make your studies both enjoyable and successful. If you can think of ways in which this could have been done more effectively, please write to tell me. In the meantime, I hope that you will gain greatly from your study of History.

Keith Randell

Acknowledgements

I would like to thank the series editor Keith Randell for his criticism of various drafts of this book. Colleagues at the University of Wolverhampton have also been extremely helpful in making this a better book. Dr Martin Durham, Dr Gerry Gomez, Pat Green and Dr Fiona Terry-Chandler all read various chapters and offered useful advice. 1 would like to thank them all. Professor John Benson made many incisive comments on the entire manuscript and I am, as ever, obliged to him for his academic generosity. Marie Wallis, an 'A' level student when this book was being written, and Hilary Bourdillon both deserve my thanks for their comments on a draft of an early chapter. I am also indebted to Professor Angela V. John who read the book carefully and made numerous helpful suggestions. My greatest thanks are to my husband, Jonathan Dudley, for his support and encouragement throughout. Any shortcomings, of course, are my own.

Chapter 1 of this book is a development of articles which first appeared in *Secondary Issues*, (ILEA, 1982) and *Teaching History*, July 1988.

The Publishers would like to thank the following for permission to reproduce illustrations in this volume:

Cover - *The Morning Paper* by Haynes King courtesy of Christie's Images; Sidgwick and Jackson, p. 23; Hulton-Deutsch, p. 34; Hodder and Stoughton archive, p. 58; The Garman Ryan Collection. Walsall Museum and Art Gallery, p. 79; Fotomas Index, p. 111; The Museum of London, p. 124; The British Library, p. 124.

Introduction: Issues and Trends in Women's History

'I can read poetry and plays, and things of that sort, and do not dislike travel. But history, real solemn history, I cannot be interested in. Can you?'
'Yes, I am fond of history.'
'I wish I were too. I read it a little as a duty, but it tells me nothing that does not either vex or weary me. The quarrels of popes and kings, with wars or pestilences, in every page; the men are all so good for nothing, and hardly any women at all - it is very tiresome.'
(Jane Austen, *Northanger Abbey*)

Until relatively recently, history was just as Jane Austen described: it was about high politics, war and diplomacy. Women, excluded from published works, school, college and university courses, were hidden from history. Today, this has changed. Women's history is, at last, a growing part of the public consciousness. Although women's history remains a minority study, there are now whole sections in bookshops devoted to women's history, it is enshrined in the National Curriculum and courses are on offer at most British universities. This chapter will examine the development of women's history in Britain and discuss the various political perspectives within it. It will show how theories of history can at times underpin research by giving examples which will be discussed in greater detail later on in the book.

One of the most exciting challenges to conventional history has been the growth of women's history. This process began quite modestly, fostered by the growth of the women's liberation movement in the 1970s and new directions in social history. The women's movement created a climate which encouraged women to challenge traditional history and coincided with the growth of oppositional history - labour history, oral history and local history - which widened the range of history in general.

Inspired by the women's movement, feminists questioned the male bias in history, women's invisibility and argued for a reappraisal of history. They claimed that history was built around the ascendancy of the male since historical knowledge originated from a powerful group in British society: the white man. Within universities, male professors explained the male historical past and encouraged their doctoral students to ratify it in their research programmes. As a consequence, more than 50 per cent of the world (i.e. women) were largely absent. Feminists maintained that this type of history was not only inadequate but inaccurate because it portrayed only a partial view of the world. It was even suggested that historical objectivity was male subjectivity.

The growth of women's history was also influenced by the growth of social and labour history and the oppositional history of the 1960s as reflected by *History Workshop* and other journals. Social historians generated an interest in women's history by expanding research into previously uncharted areas: the family, demographic trends, witchcraft and education were amongst the topics considered. These subjects offered the feminist historian further opportunities to extend women's history. Moreover, many social historians favoured a Marxist approach which further emphasised the study of subordinate groups such as the working class and women.

There is, however, no one women's history. Indeed, to explain the nature of women's history is to enter an interpretive labyrinth. The historiography of women's past, as one historian has remarked, is extraordinarily diverse both in content, methods and interpretation. There are said to be three different but interlocking strands: the herstory type of women's history, feminist history and gender history and it is these which will be considered in the next section. Nevertheless, it is important not to view these categories as inflexible as many historians use all these different approaches.

Women's history has been used as an umbrella term to cover both feminist history and gender history but it has also enjoyed its own methodology and subject matter. At one level, the herstory type of women's history is recovery or compensation history whereby previously invisible women are rescued from the past to be slotted into an already existing story. Books featuring women who have succeeded in a male world tend to be characteristic of this type of history. Biographies on women achievers, ranging from Dorothea Beale, Florence Nightingale to Mary Seacole, represent this genre.

To its credit, this approach demonstrated that women have made a significant contribution to the past. No longer can it be said that women have no history. However, this type of history remained a romp through politics and power in which famous women were added on to an already long list of powerful men. In many ways, women's history merely augmented the traditional history of 'high politics, war and diplomacy' - it did not change the way history was written. There were few 'baddies', that is women who participated in corrupt and harmful events, in this heroic version of the past. In addition, the emphasis placed on high achievers - mainly middle-class white women - meant that the lives of the majority of women who lived very ordinary lives remained unrecorded. This strengthens the belief that great individuals, rather than groups of people, made history. Furthermore, this type of women's history tended to be descriptive, aiming to recount the story of the past rather than engage with the newer and more intellectually challenging, theoretical debates of history. More importantly perhaps, women's history remained a marginal study researched and read by a committed few.

In contrast, feminist history was characterised by politics rooted in the polemics of the women's movement. As one historian has noted, feminist historians began with the premise that women were oppressed and must fight to end that oppression. History was thus a tool which was used to explain sexual inequality through the ages. It was intended to act as a means of empowerment by charting women's successful struggles against masculine domination. Just as there was no one woman's history, however, so there was no one feminist politics. In the 1970s and early 1980s there were two main groups of feminists, socialist feminists and radical feminists, who at times, fought fierce intellectual battles about the primacy of class over gender.

Socialist feminists adopted a Marxist approach whereby class remained the dominant explanation for women's oppression. Class, some believed, was more important than gender. For example, working-class women shared more in common with working-class men than with middle class women because, as members of the working class, they encountered similar economic difficulties. Working-class men and women were seen to be considerably less privileged than middle-class women because they earned less money and owned less property. Indeed, a few socialist feminists favoured an economic determinism which insisted that women's oppression stemmed from capitalism. Once socialism replaced capitalism, it was alleged, women would be liberated because socialism heralded sexual as well as class equality.

Socialist feminists often researched topics which illustrated working-class women's struggles. One example of this genre is Liddington and Norris's excellently researched book, *One Hand Tied Behind Us,* which drew attention to a previously neglected field of suffrage history: the Lancashire campaigns for votes for women. Previous historians had concentrated on the militant campaigns of the Women's Social and Political Union (WSPU), known as the suffragettes, rather than the peaceful suffragist movement. Highly critical of the suffragettes, Liddington and Norris document the participation of working-class women in the suffrage movement as a whole and offer a different version of suffrage history than that based on the story of the WSPU. As a result, suffrage history has ceased to be viewed as a predominantly middle-class movement but one in which women from all classes participated.

On the other hand, many radical feminists tended to view patriarchy, defined as the power of men over women, as the fundamental oppression facing women. Patriarchy, rather than capitalism, was perceived as the biggest obstacle to female liberation. Indeed, some of the early radical feminists placed an emphasis on biological - as opposed to economic - determinism which considered women to be different from, and sometimes superior to, men. By placing an emphasis on the essential qualities of women, radical feminists believed that women - whatever their class, colour or creed - shared a common experience and should unite against the male enemy.

Radical feminist historians tended to investigate sexual politics rather than the world of work and stressed the unity of, rather than the differences between, women of different classes. All women, it was alleged, faced a common male oppressor. Thus, in the provocatively titled *The Spinster and her Enemies*, Sheila Jeffreys challenged previous historians who viewed the nineteenth century social purity movement as a evangelical, anti-sex and repressive movement engendered by moral panic. On the contrary, Jeffreys argues, feminist social purity campaigners heralded a new dawn in sexual politics because they criticised the double standard of sexual morality and promoted a single standard of chastity for both men and women.

Whatever the theoretical position of feminists, they shared a similar weakness with those writing the herstory type of women's history. There was a common assumption in these approaches that women were to be added on to an already large bulging body of knowledge. Although writing a feminist history of women made a contribution to the totality of history it did not go far enough. As one historian has noted, adding women on to history substitutes women for men but, as with women's history, does not rewrite the past.

Although the inclusion of women into history can revitalise the subject this is not enough. The history of women should not just be about slotting women into a pre-existing framework but should raise fundamental questions about the nature of the subject. The success of women's history must be judged by its integration into traditional history and must help transform the way in which the past is viewed.

The development of gender history provided feminist historians with new insights into the past. The identification and use of the category of gender in the 1970s was an important breakthrough for feminist scholarship because it provided historians with the means by which to analyse relationships between women and men. The category of gender therefore constitutes one of the most important insights into historical understanding since the development of the category of class. It is said to have been first used by American feminists who rejected the biological determinism associated with the word 'sex'. Unlike the category 'sex' which has anatomical and biological connotations, gender was seen to be a social construct. For example, whereas men and women were quite naturally physically different, behaviour was thought to be learnt. In the early part of the nineteenth century, middle-class girls were taught how to play the piano and sew a pretty sampler. In contrast, their brothers were taught Latin and Greek. Not surprisingly, women grew up to be home-makers whereas men, intellectually more developed, were better suited to the world of work.

Gender, as a tool of historical analysis, has been utilised by some feminist historians for a number of reasons. Firstly, concern was expressed that women's history was too exclusive because it focussed narrowly on the concerns of one sex. Women's history in ignoring 50 per cent of the population fell into the same historical trap as men's history.

The category of gender offered a way forward because it offered a relational rather than a segregated category by showing that men and women were bound together in the same story rather than playing their parts in separate ones. Secondly, gender made women's history safe. It reduced the tension between feminist and other historians by containing women's history within the parameters of the historical tradition. Research concerning women and men was no longer necessarily antagonistic as both shared a common past.

Thirdly, gender history, unlike other women's history, can transform the writing of the past because it improves historical understanding. Like class, it offers a new way of analysing the historical world. It is a methodological tool which can be used to examine all historical formations as it is, like class, a fundamental organising principle of society. The category of gender provides a means by which to examine all historical social relationships, including the study of how masculinity was formed as well as the study of predominantly male institutions such as the armed forces, the judiciary and stockbroking. Gender therefore can encompass the history of the powerful as well as the powerless often favoured by social historians.

Fourthly, the category of gender enables the historian to move away from historical explanations which favour an ultimate determinant. The development of the category of gender coincided with the growth of post-structuralist history. Post-structuralists, as the name suggests, reject the overarching structural theories of class and patriarchy put forward by socialist and radical feminists in favour of an argument which asserts that power is exercised through dispersed power networks. Post-structuralists suggest that there is no one overarching theory such as class and patriarchy but a series of competing, sometimes complementary but always fluctuating categories which are continuously negotiated. In addition, post-structuralists suggest that other categories - locality, race, ethnicity, age, religion - are equally important ways of analysing the past.

Class, for example, is one of a number of different ways in which power is negotiated. Similarly, it is seen to be equally futile to produce a grand theory of female oppression because women differ across cultures, societies and time. The category of gender, with its emphasis on fluctuating power, therefore offered a bridge between the polarities of socialist and radical feminism.

Thus a new tradition is rapidly growing in which the concept of gender is used as an analytical tool with which to understand the process of history. Exciting radical perspectives were offered on the rise of industrial capitalism when the category of gender was used historically. One of the most important books to date has been *Family Fortunes* by Davidoff and Hall which uses the categories of gender, class and religion to analyse the formation of the middle class in nineteenth-century England. Hall and Davidoff put gender at the centre of their book starting from the premise that identity is gendered and that the organisation of sexual difference is central to the social world. They demonstrate how family networks provided the essential support for the rise of the middle-class male entrepreneur and ultimately the rise of the middle class as a whole.

In this type of research, gender moves beyond the task of rediscovery and beyond the bolt-on approach to the past. It untidies, disorganises and unravels the well-knit narrative of men's ideas and activities. Nonetheless there has been much criticism about the use of gender as an analytical category. Some feminists express concern that the category of gender depoliticises women's history because it deflects attack from the principle of unmasking oppression. Gender, it is argued, can be a false tool which builds shaky bridges between women and men without recognising that men ultimately hold and exert the power. In addition, gender looks as peculiarly white as other forms of women's history. Historians of the nineteenth century stress the 'cult of domesticity', the separation of the public and the private and the quest for political and economic emancipation much of which was outside the experience of a large number of black women.

Women's history is consequently in a state of flux. No one political perspective dominates the field, though the gendered perspective is the most favoured. On the contrary, women's history is characterised by a theoretical and empirical diversity which provides a challenge to orthodox ideas about objectivity in history and leaves us with the most fundamental question of all - What is history?

Making notes on *'Introduction: Issues and Trends in Women's History'*

This chapter has introduced you to the history of women's history and to the major perspectives within it. The most important point of which you should be aware is that women's history is diverse. Notes arranged under the following headings will help guide you through this difficult and complex topic.
1. Why it emerged
a) emergence of the women's liberation movement
b) development of social history
You should be aware that women's history developed out of a particular historical and political context.
2. Complex nature of women's history
a) women's history
b) feminist history
    i.   socialist feminist history
    ii. radical feminist history
    iii. gender history
You should be aware of the strengths and weaknesses of each of these perspectives and be able to cite examples based on your own reading.

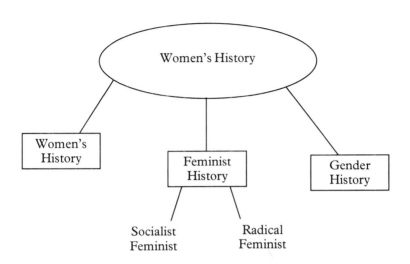

Summary - Introduction: Issues and Trends in Women's History

Answering questions on *'Introduction: Issues and Trends in Women's History'*

1 Choose two history books to discuss the following questions:
a) Are the authors, contributors, editors men or women?
b) How many men and women are named on the contents page?
c) How many men and women are in the index?
d) How many times are women mentioned in the text? Do they appear as independent people or as dependents? Are they shown in a wide range of activities or limited to stereotypes (e.g. housewives, spinners, social reformers)? Are they described in the same way as men?
e) Does the language subordinate women (e.g. a farmer and his wife, the working classes and their wives)?
f) Does the subject matter emphasise war, diplomacy and high politics or family life, work, housing, local politics, living standards? What might such an emphasis mean?

CHAPTER 2

Marriage, Home and the Family

There is too little published work on marriage, home and the family to build up much of an historiographical picture but it is fair to suppose that family history has been the concern of social historians as much as feminist ones. Histories of marriage and the family, be they written by social or feminist historians, are largely characterised by an empirical, yet critical, approach to the history of women. Most of them tell the story of women's family relationships in the nineteenth century rather than construct a theoretical argument based on the categories of class and gender. Empirical work, however, provides the historian with an evidential base from which to construct a theoretical framework. This chapter will examine a few of the key debates surrounding women and the family. It will analyse why women married, examine courtship and marriage patterns, property laws, and divorce reform. Finally it will assess the reasons for the decline in family size. In many ways, an analysis which employs the categories of both gender and class provides the best framework for women's marital position in the nineteenth century because it acknowledges the contradictions within this period.

1 Marriage

a) Why People Married

Falling in love may well have motivated people to get married in the nineteenth century but it does not provide the historian with sufficient reason for the high marriage rates of the time as compared to the present day. Marriage remained popular in the nineteenth century for a number of reasons. Most importantly, as children grew up they probably came to assume that everybody married as from the 1850s approximately 87 per cent of people wed in each generation. Marriage was perceived to be the natural order of events: it made sexual relationships permissible, ensured the legitimacy of children and provided a framework of support for the family.

Marriage was considered to be an important career prospect for women. For the majority it was an economic necessity because most women in nineteenth-century Britain found it extremely difficult to live on their own. Prevented from gaining a decent education, barred from most professions, often discouraged from working, poorly paid and without a personal income, many women married because it was virtually the only economically viable alternative to destitution - often irrespective of class background. Spinsterhood placed the majority of working-class women in an economically precarious position because wages were insufficient to maintain them. It was difficult for single women to live independently as most female jobs paid well below subsistence level. Wages, even in the highly paid cotton mills, did not provide sufficient income to enable single women to live alone. Governesses, the occupation of the genteel poor, were equally poorly paid and could not afford to live adequately on their salary. Richer women might be supported by their families - and there was a significant minority of influential spinsters in the nineteenth century - but for the vast majority, marriage provided an opportunity of living comfortably.

For the upper classes, marriage was an important social institution which merged property as much as people. For a young woman with a fortune, title and land it was crucial that she make a good match to secure her family property for generations to come. A great deal of attention was paid to the marrying of daughters because of the potential alliances which could be made with other influential families. Young working-class girls, especially of the upper class were regarded as expensive goods and chattels to be displayed and 'sold' to the highest 'bidder'. One young woman, at a painting exhibition, said to her grandmother 'I think, we young ladies in the world, when we are exhibiting, ought to have little green tickets pinned on our backs, with 'Sold' written on them; it would prevent trouble and any future haggling. Then at the end of the season the owner would come to carry us home'. Middle-class families, although not so wealthy, viewed marriage in a similar way. In mid-Victorian Birmingham inter-marriage between the ruling Nonconformist clique ensured that a small family network remained powerful in local politics. Marriage, or at least a permanent partner, was equally important for the working class but their choice was regulated by different principles. Wives were chosen as much for the wealth they brought to marriage as for their domestic abilities, their craft skills and their ability to bear children.

For most women, marriage was significantly better than the alternative as spinsters were referred to, somewhat unflatteringly, as 'surplus' or 'redundant' women who had been 'left on the shelf'. Novels of the period reflect this fear by depicting sad, old spinsters trapped at home, bowing to the whims of elderly parents. Unmarried women were marginalised in Victorian and Edwardian England and often faced an isolated and somewhat lonely existence in the household of a relative where they were expected to help with the management of the household. Rich single heiresses like Florence Nightingale and Angela Burdett-Coutts were the exception and were protected from public scorn by their achievements and good works as much as their wealth.

b) Courtship Patterns and Marriage Ceremonies

Courtship was regulated in quite distinct ways within each class. Relationships between the sexes of the upper class were very carefully controlled because marriage was an important economic venture. By the middle of the nineteenth century marriage had ceased to be arranged in the more formal sense but parents still ensured that daughters met suitable partners. The lives of women under 30 were severely restricted: they could not go unchaperoned to theatres, dances or restaurants. Coming-out parties ensured that young women met others from an equally desirable background. The season in London, alongside country house parties, was viewed by mothers and daughters as a suitable marriage market because upper-class girls were likely to meet socially desirable young men in the balls, parties and theatres that they all frequented.

Once the serious intentions of the suitor were voiced, and more importantly accepted, the courting process of the upper class was rigidly controlled. Courtship was not a secret romantic private affair but a public event which was witnessed by families, friends and relatives; and the elaborate rules of courtship imposed upon young people ensured that the family rarely relinquished control. A young woman was never left alone in a room with an unrelated male but was accompanied at all times by a married gentlewoman or a servant. Neither a kiss nor a cuddle was allowed between courting couples. This was not for reasons of propriety alone but because parents wished their daughters to remain sexually ignorant until marriage because of the fear of illegitimacy. No upper-class or middle-class man wanted to take on children that had been fathered by someone else.

Working-class people chose their own partners but they were limited in other ways. It was unlikely that young women would choose partners from outside their social and geographical group. Harvest time, feast days, fairs and wakes provided opportunities to meet the opposite sex but most young women married within their own local network. In the early nineteenth century in one small village in Devon, 65 per cent of all marriages were within the village while in some areas it was frowned upon if men courted women from a different place. However, by the end of the century this was less so, especially among the skilled, better-off working class.

Virginity was not so highly prized amongst the working class, at least in the first half of the century. In contrast to upper- and middle-class experience, some working-class communities practised 'bundling', a procedure where the couple spent the night together, fully clothed, and engaged in heavy petting. Sex before marriage or premarital pregnancy was accepted in rural communities. Marriage, in some country districts, did not occur until the women became pregnant because men had no wish to marry 'a pig in a poke'. In one northern weaving town, 90 per cent of first births were conceived outside of marriage in the first half of the century. The following extract from Dorset sums it all up:

1 The mode of courtship here, is that a young woman never admits of the serious addresses of a young man but on the supposition of a thorough probation. When she becomes with child, she tells her

mother; the mother tells her father; her father tells his father, and
5 he tells his son, that it is the proper time to be married. ... If the
woman does not prove with child, after a competent time of
courtship, they conclude they are not destined by Providence for
each other; they therefore separate.

Marriage ceremonies differed, at least in the first half of the nineteenth
century. Until 1837, when Roman Catholics and Nonconformists were
given licences to celebrate marriage, couples, apart from Quakers and
Jews, had to get married in an Anglican church to make sure that their
children were considered legitimate. Even so, not everyone married
within the law as some did not wish to pay the cost of legal marriage.
Marriage licences cost between five and twelve old shillings which was
up to three days' wages for many working-class people. Some at the
lower end of the working class did not bother with a legal ceremony.
Irregular forms of marriage took place amongst some groups: jumping
the broom, was a popular method in a few country districts; London
shoemakers exchanged handkerchiefs. Costermongers (food-sellers)
rarely bothered to marry at all - a survey by Mayhew in the 1840s
indicated that only one in ten bothered to pay for a formal ceremony,
considering it a unnecessary extravagance. Other working-class people
lived in permanent relationships. A survey by the London City Mission
in 1848 reported that 500 out of 700 couples in Westminster were not
legally married even though they may have lived together for some time.

2 Marriage and Property Laws

Once married, women lost their legal status. In 1815 the law stipulated
that husband and wife were one, and that the 'one' was the husband.
Considered the chattels or possession of their husbands, women
suffered from a chain of legislative inequality. Husbands had the right to
decide where to live and how to live, they were legally entitled to, and
sometimes did, beat their wives and could, and sometimes did, lock
them up. Once divorced, husbands gained custody of all children.
Property laws underpinned this iniquitous legislation.

In 1815, married women were constrained by two branches of
property law - common law and the equity law - which dispensed very
different types of marital justice. Once married, women had few legal
rights in common law. They were considered to be the property of their
husband who also owned the home and everything within it, all their
earnings, their belongings, clothes, stocks, shares and money. Husbands
could dispose of this wealth as they thought fit - even if husband and wife
no longer lived together. Moreover, wives could not sue, sign contracts,
run a business or make a will without the permission of their husbands.
On the other hand, some advantage accrued to women on marriage
because wives could not be sued, husbands were liable for any debt

accumulated by their wives - even if women ordered goods without the knowledge of the husband, the latter was obliged to pay the cost. The following three cases demonstrate the injustices of common law. One working-class wife, who had set up a profitable laundry business, on being deserted by her husband was left penniless when he returned many years later to demand her hard-earned money. At the other end of the economic spectrum, Caroline Norton's aristocratic husband, George, sequestered all of Caroline's earnings from her writing as well as money inherited from her mother, after they had separated. Even well-known feminists suffered. When Mrs Fawcett, leader of the suffrage movement, had her purse stolen she was surprised to hear the thief charged in court with 'stealing from the person of Millicent Fawcett a purse containing £1 18s 6d, the property of Henry Fawcett'.

Equity law was quite different. Under equity law, marriage settlements were drawn up by solicitors to protect the property of the family against spendthrift sons-in-law. Capital was held in trust for the children of the marriage: wives were only able to draw interest upon it. Nevertheless equity law gave women considerable financial independence as all money received from these trusts belonged to the wives and they were free to spend it as they wished. As capital accrued interest at roughly 4 per cent, a few married women had quite considerable financial freedom. If their wives predeceased them, husbands were entitled to draw interest on the capital to pay for the upkeep of the children but the estate reverted to the children of the marriage after the death of their father or when they reached maturity.

However, only a small minority, approximately 10 per cent of families, took advantage of equity law. Marriage settlements were complex affairs which required the expertise of solicitors, making it an expensive procedure which only the most wealthy could afford. Rich, aristocratic parents, concerned about profligate sons-in-law, used equity not to protect their daughters but to ensure that the family wealth was not squandered by dissolute husbands.

Most parents could not afford equity and were governed by common law. Middle-class women were also disadvantaged by property laws because many had disposable incomes but could not afford the costly settlements or trusts of the aristocracy. Consequently, all inheritance and earned income was transferred to husbands on marriage. Women were forbidden to dispose of their own inherited property or earned income without their husbands' permission. At the other end of the economic spectrum working-class women, who made up three-quarters of the female population, were equally unable to pay the legal costs involved.

This system changed in 1870 when the Married Woman's Property Act (MWPA) gave women the right to keep their own earnings, their personal property, income from some investments, rents and profits from land, and money under £200 bequeathed to them. There was a number of reasons why the 1870 MWPA was passed. Firstly it was passed to correct a legal anomaly; secondly powerful pressure groups campaigned to reform the law; and thirdly the timing was politically advantageous. These reasons will be considered in greater detail below.

The MWPA was passed to fill a legal loophole by extending the rights already held by the aristocratic rich to the rest of the population. Concern was expressed that there was one law for the very rich, who were the only ones who could afford equity, and another law for everyone else. Upper-class married women had some control over their own property through equity law but most women did not. Middle-class and working-class women, it was believed, should be offered the same protection in law as the upper class. The MWPA was therefore passed in order to end the disparity between equity law and common law.

Legal anomalies can and do remain on the statute books for years. It generally requires the hard work of individuals or pressure groups to persuade governments to remedy injustices. Historians agree that feminists set reform of the Property Laws as their major priority. There is little doubt that feminist campaigners, along with their male supporters, created the moral climate in which reform could take place. Feminists argued that by depriving women of property it divested them of a legal existence because married women were unable to own property or sign contracts and were thus unable to engage in business or trade. It was claimed that married women were categorised alongside criminals, lunatics and children because they were not considered competent enough or responsible enough to manage their own affairs.

The experience of Caroline Norton (briefly mentioned on page 12) was used to support their case and coalesced public opinion. Caroline Norton, a famous society beauty, had legally separated from her husband, George, but was still tied to him economically. Even though the couple lived apart, George Norton legally sequestrated all of Caroline's earnings from her writings as well as her inherited wealth. One historian has noted that the case of Caroline Norton provided the impetus for the campaign to reform the property laws because of the perceived gross injustice of her situation.

Laws, however, are made and amended by Parliament. By 1869, the year before the 1870 MWPA was passed, the political climate was transformed by a newly elected Liberal Government committed to limited reform. Many Liberal MPs supported the MWPA because they believed that it might compensate for not giving women the vote. This was because it was believed that one of the reasons why women wanted the vote was to redress the injustice of the property laws. Once the property laws had been rationalised in favour of all women it was thought that the demand for women's suffrage might disappear. As a result of Liberal Party support, the passage of the MWPA was secured but the Lords amended the proposed Act to such an extent that it became a shadow of its former legal self.

Historians have sometimes viewed the MWPA as an important milestone in women's emancipation and the most important legal reform for women in the nineteenth century. It certainly altered the distribution of wealth in England as every married woman in the country now had ownership and control of her earnings, savings and inheritance. The passing of the 1870 Act was also seen to have had a deep psychological effect on women who now believed themselves to be independent beings with rights and control over their own money, at least in law. The MWPA broke women's financial dependency on their husbands and allowed them to spend their own money as they wished. With new-found economic independence, and their own money in their own pockets, wives were encouraged to develop their own interests. As a result, the marriage relationship was modified. By the end of the century marriage was more companionable than it had been at the beginning and the 'angel in the house' had ceased to be an ideal image.

In addition the MWPA allegedly gave women a sense of achievement and a confidence that they could fight and win. The feminist organisations inspired by the MWPA continued to campaign for further reforms. And, perhaps more importantly, the practical experience gained in organising petitions, writing leaflets and speaking in public was later used in other political movements. However, not all of this was the result of the MWPA: to a large extent the 1870 Act reflected rather than promoted changes in women's position. The MWPA was passed at a time when women were beginning to make inroads into the masculine world of work and politics, which in turn gave them the confidence to demand more equal treatment in law.

However, the MWPA was merely an extension of the rights held by the upper class (through the law of equity) to the middle class (through the common law). Moreover, both the Equity and the common laws protected family wealth rather than women, for although the 1870 Act gave women and their families minimal protection against avaricious husbands it did not give married women the same status as single women. These rights were extended in further Property Acts, which are mentioned in the chronology, but married women had to wait until 1935 to enjoy the same status as single women.

3 Divorce

Until the nineteenth century most marriages rarely lasted more than 20 years because one partner died at a fairly early age but with increased longevity people stayed married for much longer. Little by little, divorce reform allowed unhappily married couples to separate yet divorce remained difficult for upper-class men, doubly so for middle-class men and almost impossible for women.

Before the Divorce Act of 1857 divorce was extremely rare and only possible for wealthy men. If a couple wished to divorce they had to secure a Private Act of Parliament which was an expensive (estimated at £475 in the first half of the century) and extremely time consuming ordeal because it involved three different lawsuits. Before proceedings could take place in Parliament, husbands had to obtain a separation order from an ecclesiastical court and a verdict against their wives for adultery, called criminal conversation, in a common law court. Grounds for divorce were tougher for women, and without an independent income or family support, impossible to enact. Whereas men had to prove adultery, women also had to prove gross cruelty, bigamy or incest. Not surprisingly, very few people took advantage of this limited licence: between 1765 and 1857 only 276 divorces were granted. Only four of these were to women.

Because of the difficulties in obtaining a divorce, wealthy people took advantage of other legal procedures to end an unhappy marriage. There were three main ways in which this could be achieved (the first two of which could also be used as preparation for a full divorce). The first method was a judicial separation by the ecclesiastical, as opposed to the civil courts. In cases of sodomy and cruelty, wives were granted legal separation and obtained generous alimony. By contrast, if wives were found guilty of adultery they were left penniless. Ecclesiastical courts could also - and often did - declare marriages null and void: a claim of bigamy or non-consummation could be used to end a marriage even though any children of such a union were declared illegitimate.

Alternatively, husbands were able to sue other men in the civil court for 'criminal conversation'. As wives were considered the property of their husbands, jealous spouses were able to sue other men for trespass. By committing adultery, defendants had used the body of a wife and had thus damaged the property of husbands. It was a particularly vengeful Act as those accused paid high costs: sometimes as much as £20,000. For victorious husbands, a suit of criminal conversation was a lucrative pursuit but for convicted adulterers it meant a huge dent in their income, perhaps penury or life imprisonment if they were unable to pay damages. One particularly unsavoury case involved people at the pinnacle of the social and political hierarchy. In the 1830s George Norton sued the Prime Minister, Lord Melbourne, for criminal conversation with his wife, Caroline. George lost the case and with it the chance of a divorce through Act of Parliament but Caroline lost much more: her reputation.

Finally, separation by private deed enabled a marriage to be terminated. It benefited women because it evaded the public humiliation of divorce, endowed separated wives with one-third of their husbands' net income, enabled them to live as a single person and even gave them the right to live with another man should they so wish.

Legal divorce, and of course these other devices, was virtually impossible for the working class who sometimes used other methods. Leaving home and working a few miles away enabled husbands to circumvent the courts and sometimes remarry. Husbands who absconded from unhappy marriages often left their deserted wives with dependent children, without alimony or means to survive. Wife selling occurred in the early years of the nineteenth century but, like divorce, was rarely employed. Between 1780-1880 there were only 294 recorded cases of wife sales in England. One wife was brought to Walsall market to be sold in 1837:

1 They came into the market between ten and eleven o'clock in the morning, the woman being led by a halter, which was fastened round her neck and the middle of her body. In a few minutes after their arrival she was sold to a man of the name of Thomas Snape, a
5 nailer, also of Burntwood. There were not many people in the market at the time. The purchase money was 2s 6d and all the parties seemed satisfied with the bargain.

In theory the wife was treated like a slave who could be bought and sold but in reality the woman (called Mrs Hitchinson) had been living with Mr Snape for three years so this may well have been a working-class form of divorce and remarriage. Wife selling was also a way of gaining approval and community acceptance of an already established liaison. Although not legally binding, the sale transferred financial responsibility from the husband to the lover as under this arrangement wives could not run up debts against their separated husband nor claim any estate on his death. On the other hand, the husband could not sue his separated wife's lover for criminal conversation or sequester her goods.

By mid century this system changed because of new legislation. The Divorce Act of 1857 is often viewed as a watershed in legal history since it established civil divorce for the first time. However, this reform did not introduce any new principles of divorce but just altered the way in which the law was administered as it really only benefited wealthy men and continued to reflect the gender and class inequalities of nineteenth-century England.

By 1900 only 582 people had obtained a divorce because of a number of weaknesses in the new Act. There was only one divorce court and this was in London which made it difficult for people living in provincial districts to petition for divorce. Divorce proceedings remained expensive and out of the financial reach of most people. In addition, there continued to be one law for men and a different law for women. Divorce law is a good example of the sexual double standard of Victorian England for distinctly unequal moral standards applied to each of the sexes. Under the new legislation men were able to divorce their wives for adultery. On the other hand, women's access to divorce was limited: the adulterous husband had to commit either bigamy, rape, sodomy, bestiality, cruelty or long-term desertion before the long suffering wife could petition for divorce. Women were expected to forgive and forget an adulterous husband whereas a wife who indulged in extra-marital sexual intercourse removed herself from respectable society and put herself in the category of 'fallen woman'. Female adultery, it was believed, so threatened the sanctity of marriage and challenged the legitimacy of children that tighter controls were put on women than on men. This was justified because the wife's adultery threatened inheritance and property rights whereas the man's did not as the Lord Chancellor was quick to point out in 1857:

1 A wife might, without any loss of caste ... condone an act of adultery on the part of her husband; but a husband could not condone a similar act on the part of a wife. No one would venture to suggest that a husband could possibly do so ... the adultery of
5 the wife might be the means of palming spurious offspring upon the husband, while the adultery of the husband could have no such effect with regard to the wife.

It was not until 1923 that women and men were granted similar divorce rights.

4 The Decline in Family Size

Britain is rapidly becoming a country of old people. This, according to social commentators, affects the ratio between the number of people of working age and those in retirement. It is feared that there will not be enough people in work to support those drawing their state pension. One reason for this is the rapid fall in the number of children being born. This crisis has been over a hundred years in the making.

Industrialisation triggered major changes in British domestic life which in turn affected family size. A long-term reason for the decline in family size was the separation of the world of work from the world of the home. As a consequence of this separation, the home changed from being a unit of production to a unit of consumption. Higher aspirations, an increased standard of living and an expectation of a comfortable home life in turn led to a decline in the birth rate in the latter part of the century. Children, no longer part of the productive economy, became increasingly expensive. At the same time, new methods of contraception offered women the opportunity to control their fertility. In addition, the increased risks of childbirth may have deterred many women from pregnancy. These reasons will be considered in greater detail in the next section.

a) Changes in the Home

By separating the home from the world of work, industrialisation confirmed women's role as home maker. It might be expected that the growth of women staying at home would have led to an increase, rather than a decrease, in the birth rate but this was not the case. On the contrary, industrialisation led to, or at least was associated with, a decline - in the long term - in family size.

The separation of home and work resulted in the home changing from a centre of production to one of consumption, making the home a place where money was spent rather than made. Historians have suggested that when middle-class women withdrew from the productive sphere they played an increasingly important role in the development of the consumer society. Women were new consumers who had the time, energy and commitment to spend any surplus income. Advertisements tried to persuade middle-class women to buy the latest goods made available by innovative technology. Cast iron ranges (which provided heating, cooking facilities and hot water and could be removed when the owner moved house) replaced open fires, the use of gas, the development of the soap industry, the introduction of piped water all raised standards of cleaning, cooking and washing. When gas cookers, which could be hired by those who could ill afford to buy one, were introduced in the 1880s they gradually overtook the open range. Carpets, upholstered furniture, decorative objects all helped to make the home a comfortable place in which to live. Middle-class people found these improvements costly so were willing to limit the size of their families in order to afford this new-found luxury.

For middle- and upper-class women running a home was like managing a small hotel, especially when they had numerous domestic servants to supervise, large amounts of food to buy, guests to entertain and household budgets to balance. Dinner parties, an important middle-class social activity, demanded forward planning, an organised kitchen, a well-served table and a pleasing hostess. Isabella Beeton wrote *Beeton's Book of Household Management* to guide married women through their daily lives:

1 As with the Commander of an Army, or the leader of any enterprise, so it is with the mistress of a house. Her spirit will be seen through the whole establishment; and just in proportion as she performs her duties intelligently and thoroughly, so will her
5 domestics follow in her path. Of all those acquirements, which more particularly belong to the feminine character, there are none which take a higher rank, in our estimation, than such as enter into a knowledge of household duties; for on these are perpetually dependent the happiness, comfort, and well-being of a family.
10   Having risen early ... and having given due attention to the bath, and made a careful toilet, it will be well at once to see that the children have received their proper ablutions, and are in every way clean and comfortable.

After breakfast is over, it will be well for the mistress to make a
15 round of the kitchen and other offices, to see that all are in order,
and that the morning's work has been properly performed by the
various domestics. The orders for the day should then be given ...
    After luncheon visits may be made and received ... Visits of
20 ceremony, or courtesy ... are uniformly required after dining at a
friend's house, or after a ball ... The morning calls being paid or
received, and their etiquette properly attended to, the next great
event of the day in most establishments is 'The Dinner'.

Although middle-class women led a busy life, their work was unpaid and
did not make a profit. Indeed, middle- and upper-class women were
defined by their leisured elegance, as husbands from this particular class
wanted wives who would grace the dinner table rather than scrub a clean
floor. Perfect wives were perfect ladies: elegant, refined and socially
accomplished. They were decorative, and costly, ancillaries to their
successful working husbands rather than contributors to the family
income.

    Working-class women could not usually afford the improvements
generated by the industrial age. For the working-class women, who had
to fetch water from the stream, well or pump, domesticity took a heavier
toll. Even in the 1890s many working-class women used an open fire
and depended on the communal oven to make their bread. Cleaning was
an arduous task before the age of the vacuum cleaner as mops and
brooms were the only cleaning tools available and soap was expensive so
sand and lye, often made communally, was used as cleaning materials.
In addition, wash day for working-class women was a public occasion,
often done by the well or nearest stream rather than in the home itself.
According to some historians, children were a welcome commodity in
these homes because they could help with the cooking, cleaning,
collecting of water and general household duties. Furthermore, the
world of work and the world of home was less sharply defined for
working-class women. Most working-class men did not earn sufficient
income to keep their wives at home, let alone pay for a vast army of
domestic servants. Not surprisingly, working-class families reduced the
size of their families much later than the middle classes.

b) Cost of Children

For both middle-class and working-class families, however, children
were becoming increasingly expensive to bring up. Historians generally
agree that formal career structures combined with the rising educational
cost of male children in particular encouraged smaller families amongst
the middle and upper class. Career structures became clearly defined
amongst the professional classes and as educational qualifications
replaced older forms of patronage so it proved expensive to launch a son

into an acceptable career. More and more professions such as the law, medicine and the Church began to insist upon formal qualifications as a prerequisite for employment. In some cases it meant staying longer at expensive schools or going on to university. The great crop of new public schools founded between 1840 and 1870, such as Radley and Marlborough, reflect the new ambition to provide boys with the necessary qualifications to enter a profession.

Protective legislation which restricted child labour, combined with educational opportunities, made great demands upon the working-class family budget. In the early part of the century young children were engaged in both factory and mine work but restrictions on child labour meant that children were a declining part of the workforce. By 1876 schooling for the 5-10 age group was compulsory which contributed to a further decline of children's paid work. Some historians have assumed that because the working class viewed their children as economic assets they were willing to reduce their family size when they ceased to be so.

c) Birth Control

Later marriage used to be held responsible for the decline in the birth rate but recently historians have shifted their attention to the importance of birth control. In the first part of the nineteenth century very few people publicly advocated birth control. Not only was it perceived to interfere with God's law but some feared that birth control might increase immorality because it reduced the risk of conception. Birth control was also associated with prostitution so the use of contraceptive devices tainted women with sexual licentiousness. Others, often in the medical profession, believed that women would become seriously ill if they used contraceptives. Cancer, sterility, madness and even nymphomania, they argued, were all likely to occur as a result of birth control. By the end of the century this had changed. Birth control was, if not respectable, then quite widely available and a number of reasons are put forward for its increasing popularity.

Control over reproduction has often been linked to women's emancipation: the 1960s pill was associated with mini-skirts and sexual freedom. Some historians have argued that feminism provided much of the impetus for nineteenth-century birth control and suggest that there was a causal relationship between the emancipation of women and smaller families. However, this is not a very convincing argument as there was never just one feminist voice on birth control. Some favoured birth control because it freed women from the yearly ritual of pregnancy. Once women were emancipated from constant child bearing it was believed that they could participate fully in the economic, social and political life of the country. Other feminists were averse to birth control because they believed that it granted sexual licence to men and further diminished women's right to say no in marriage. Feminist hostility was directed against men who used women as vessels for their sexual satisfaction and the *Freewoman*, a feminist journal published in the early twentieth century, argued that contraception permitted men to overindulge their sexual passion. In spite of this ambivalence amongst feminists it can still be argued that feminism provided the backdrop against which the campaign for birth control was played.

Some historians have argued that because birth control literature was around at the beginning of the nineteenth century it must mean that birth control was much in use. In 1826, for example, Francis Place and other radical men published a book on contraceptive advice which was freely available in cotton mills. It was said that mill workers had more opportunities to disseminate this knowledge among co-workers because they worked in larger factories than most other women. Other historians have stressed that the Malthusian League, formed in 1877, provided the ideological framework for birth control. The League thought that birth control was a social necessity because the physical health and intellectual stock of the nation was diminishing due to the abundantly fecund working- class producing too many babies. Furthermore, it was believed that the working-class burdened an already laden state with unnecessary charitable expenses because they gave birth to babies they could not afford to keep. To prevent the upper and middle class from being swamped by what was perceived to be an inferior breed the Malthusian League distributed leaflets and pamphlets advocating birth control to working-class homes. Alternatively, some historians have argued that the decline in the birth rate coincided with the prosecution of Annie Besant and Charles Bradlaugh in 1877 for republishing a rather outdated book on birth control. The flood of birth control information which followed this trial was seen to be the real reason for the widespread use of contraception.

In addition, new technology helped to produce better and more effective forms of contraception. The most widely practised methods of family limitation were abstinence, coitus interruptus (the withdrawal method), prolonged lactation (breast-feeding) and abortion. At the beginning of the nineteenth century the technology of contraception was still in its infancy. The condom or rubber sheath had been made from animal intestines on the sausage-skin principle since the early eighteenth century and was used as a prevention against venereal disease. Condoms were generally used with prostitutes which explains the reluctance of the 'respectable' to use them. With the vulcanisation of rubber in 1843 animal intestines were successfully substituted by this new material. By the 1890s several firms supplied the market, Durex in particular was well-established with barbers shops acting as the major outlets. Rubber cervical caps, syringes and soluble pessaries were also popularised. However, in the 1890s it cost 10p for a sponge, 20p for a dozen condoms - still an expensive item for the poorer section of society. Advice on contraception still remained limited and the medical profession remained hostile to its adoption. Consequently, the most widely practised methods of family limitation were the natural ones: coitus interruptus or prolonged lactation which were also the least effective. Some desperate married couples even chose abstinence.

When all else failed, abortion or abortifacents were used to end an unwanted pregnancy. In 1803 abortion, after quickening, (a stage in pregnancy when movements in the fetus can be felt) became a capital offence but as with most crimes of the time which incurred a death penalty, juries were reluctant to convict. In 1837 this Act was repealed and replaced by one which made abortion punishable by maximum punishment of transportation for life or up to three years imprisonment. A variety of other punishments were given to anyone who administered medicines or used instruments to procure a miscarriage before quickening. Despite heavy penalties, herbal remedies continued to be widely advertised to procure a miscarriage. Frequent advertisements such as the one below appeared in newspapers:

Ladies only

THE LADY MONTROSE
MIRACULOUS
FEMALE TABULES

Are positively unequalled for all FEMALE AILMENTS. The most OBSTINATE obstructions, Irregularities, etc. of the female system are removed in a few doses.

Abortifacents like lead plaster, pills, a mixture of herbs, gin and salts, gunpowder, soaking nails and pennies in water and even rat poison were used in an attempt to procure the end of an unwanted pregnancy. We can never know the numbers of women who used abortifacents or abortion as a form of birth control but one historian has indicated its widespread popularity by examining an extortion trial which took place in 1898. Two brothers, called Richard and Edward Chrimes, posted 8,100 threatening letters to women who had purchased abortifacents from them. Within a few days 3,000 desperate women had replied enclosing money (a total of £819) in exchange for the Chrimes brothers' silence. Such widespread and quick response must indicate that a large number of women used abortifacents as a method of birth control. Although Richard and Edward were sentenced to 12 years for extortion there was still a lack of sympathy for women who wanted to terminate a pregnancy and abortion remained a crime until the mid twentieth century. Women who used contraception or procured abortion were in the minority, however, as the majority of women chose to continue with their pregnancy.

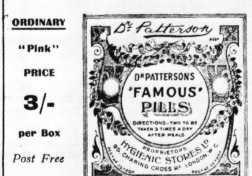

☞ **A BOON TO WOMANKIND** ☜

"Dr. PATTERSON'S"
FAMOUS PILLS
Contain no Irritative or Dangerous Drugs.
THE GREAT REMEDY FOR
IRREGULARITIES OF EVERY DESCRIPTION.

ORDINARY

"Pink"

PRICE

3/-

per Box

Post Free

Privately Packed.

FACSIMILE OF LABEL

SPECIAL

"Pink"

PRICE

5/-

per Box

Post Free

Privately Packed.

THESE PILLS were used with unvarying success in the treatment of all Ailments during Dr. PATTERSON'S 30 years experience in some of the largest Institutions abroad. They restore to their usual health, when Pennyroyal and Steel, Pil Cochiae, Bitter Apple, mixtures, pellets and tablets, etc., fail; they have the approval of the Medical Profession, and are in daily use at home and abroad. In all cases of anæmia, lassitude, melancholy, variable appetite, weakness, and debility of every description they are the **safest** and most **efficacious** medicine known; they may be safely taken at any time, and their use according to the **directions** given with each box, will quickly bring about the desired effect. The great and constantly increasing sale of these Pills is not the result of extensive advertising, but of **personal recommendation alone** (a sure test of their merits).

PERSONAL ATTENTION GIVEN TO ALL ORDERS.

Perfectly Harmless and Warranted Free from all Dangerous Drugs.

ADVICE FREE. Call or Write

THE HYGIENIC STORES LTD.,
Chemists,
95 CHARING CROSS ROAD, LONDON, W.C. 2.

Telephone: 0823 Regent.   Telegraphic Address: "Hygistor," London.

IMPORTANT NOTICE.—The Public are warned that to get the genuine Dr. Patterson's Famous Pills they should be obtained only from The Hygienic Stores Limited, 95 Charing Cross Road, London, W.C. 2. Look for Reg. No. 357207.

Left margin: Dr. PATTERSON'S COPYRIGHT LABEL—Registered No. 357207   WATCH FOR

Right margin: WATCH FOR Dr. PATTERSON'S COPYRIGHT LABEL—Registered No. 357207

'Dr Patterson's famous pills'

d) Dangers of Childbirth

Another reason for limiting family size may have been the alarming increase in maternal mortality amongst the middle class. Pregnancy and childbirth were dangerous activities for women of all classes throughout the nineteenth century - ante-natal care was primitive, childbirth painful and after-care limited - but middle-class women seemed to suffer more than working-class women from technological improvements.

Antenatal care, in practice, was virtually non-existent for all classes. Many women first saw their doctor or midwife when they booked them for their confinement as pregnancy was difficult to diagnose without an internal examination which many women were reluctant to undergo. Only the obvious signs, stopping menstruation, fullness of the breasts, morning sickness and eventually quickening of the fetus were considered to be reliable symptoms of conception. As a result most women kept their pregnancy a secret until it was fairly obvious, not because of modesty as was once assumed, but because they wanted to ensure that they really were pregnant.

Childbirth itself was dangerous and it was estimated that approximately five mothers died for every thousand children born. Giving birth to large numbers of children - sometimes 10 or 12 - obviously hastened an early death but there were other reasons. Most births in all classes took place in the home even when there were complications. Quite surprisingly husbands were present at the birth in all political families from about 1830. Indeed Prince Albert had been present when Queen Victoria gave birth in 1841 as was W.E. Gladstone at the birth of his first child. In fact, the husband's presence was commonplace until women gave birth in hospitals. Home births, however, were more dangerous for middle-class women than for the working class because they were more likely to be attended by a doctor at the birth of their child. With the professionalisation of medicine, doctors gradually replaced midwives to take over what was traditionally a female occupation: delivering babies. One of the most important changes in childbirth in the nineteenth century was the development of gynaecology and obstetrics which was a direct consequence of this professional approach. One would assume that better trained, highly educated professionals were far more suited to looking after their patients than untrained staff. However, the evidence is that doctors were no better - even with the introduction of forceps - than experienced midwives in caring for pregnant women. One historian has suggested that a disproportionate number of middle-class women died from puerperal fever (septic poisoning) as a direct consequence of poor hygiene on the part of the medical profession. Puerperal fever was the most common cause of death in the nineteenth century. (Women are prone to infection directly after giving birth because the placenta leaves a large wound in the uterus which takes about a month to heal. High standards of hygiene were essential to prevent this occurring but unfortunately for middle- and upper-class women, precautions were rarely taken. Doctors were often the major source of puerperal fever because they carried germs from their diseased patients to the women in labour. One historian has noted that the doctor '… could and did carry to the parturient woman laudable pus from his surgical cases, droplets from scarlet fever cases and putrefaction from the corpses he dissected'. In the 1840s Semmelweis, an Hungarian obstetrician, forced his staff to scrub their hands with chloride of lime before examining patients, but his advice was disregarded by many English doctors who failed even to wash their hands. Working-class women could not afford the specialised attention of a doctor so were looked after by a midwife. Women were in safer hands not because midwives were cleaner but because they were in contact with far fewer diseases. For women of all classes, however, childbirth remained a life-threatening experience until the development of blood transfusions after the First World War and antibiotics such as penicillin after the Second.

Childbirth was also a painful as well as a dangerous process even though the discovery of chloroform by James Simpson in 1847 eased it a little for middle- and upper-class women. Apparently the first woman to be administered chloroform called her daughter Anaesthesia. Queen Victoria popularised its use but it tended to be given only in harrowing and difficult labours. For working-class women there was no pain relief. Tearing in childbirth was common for all women but before 1900 these tears were either ignored or badly stitched as episiotomy (a surgical cut made in the vagina to ease delivery) was rare before the First World War. After the birth of their child middle- and upper-class women were confined to bed for a couple of weeks to rest and recover but few working-class women enjoyed such luxury.

Given the evidence charted above, it is perhaps not surprising that parents took a positive decision to limit the size of their families. Contraception, however, became popular amongst the various classes at different times. Long before the trial of Annie Besant and Charles Bradlaugh in 1877, the upper class pioneered contraception at least a good generation in advance of the rest of the population. The middle class began to limit the size of their families from about 1850 onwards. The size of the working-class family fell amongst skilled workers first of all, particularly amongst cotton workers, perhaps explained by the better employment opportunities enjoyed by such women and the greater opportunities they had to disseminate knowledge. Women gained in other ways. By 1914 women of all classes had benefited from technological developments, changes in attitude, law reform and an improved standard of living. Equality had not yet been achieved but progress, it is said, was being made.

Making notes on *'Marriage, Home and the Family'*

It is important for you to understand the analysis contained within this chapter and to think about some of the issues, particularly around class, that have been raised. You might like to think about the following questions as a focal point for your notes. Did women of the working and middle class marry for similar reasons? To what extent was there a class difference in marriage patterns? How constrained were women by the property laws of the nineteenth century? How did the double standard affect women's ability to divorce their husbands? What were the long- and short-term factors behind the decline in family size?

Source-based questions on *'Marriage, Home and the Family'*

1 The Nature of Marriage
Read the extract on page1 10-11 about courtship. Answer the following questions.
a) What does the writer mean by 'the supposition of a thorough probation'? (2 marks)

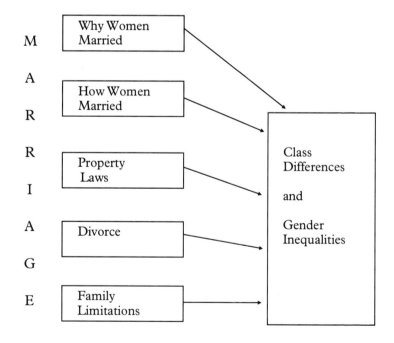

Summary - Marriage, Home and the Family

b) What does this source tell the historian about courtship patterns? (3 marks)
c) To what extent were premarital relationships different between the working and middle classes? (5 marks)

2 Adultery

Read the extract on page 17 about adultery. Answer the following questions.
a) What is meant by palming spurious offspring? (2 marks)
b) What does this speech tell the historian about the sexual double standards? (3 marks)
c) How representative was the Lord Chancellor of male opinion? (5 marks)

3 Domesticity

Read the extract from Isabella Beeton's book on pages 10-19. Answer the following questions.
a) What are the chief tasks, according to Beeton, of a married woman? (3 marks)
b) What does this extract tell the historian about the perceived role of women at this time? (4 marks)
c) How far is Isabella Beeton's ideal from the reality of the nineteenth century? (6 marks)

4 An Advertisement for Abortifacents

Read the advert for Dr Patterson's pills on page 23. Answer the following questions.
a) What evidence is there in this advert that Dr Patterson's pills might be used to procure an abortion? (4 marks)
b) What advertising methods were used to persuade women to buy these pills? (3 marks)

CHAPTER 3

The Gendering of Education

Today every child in Britain has the right to free state education until the age of 16. In 1800 it was quite different as the majority of children never went to school. By the end of the nineteenth century this had changed as a range of schools stretched across the British Isles providing education for all. The rapid and impressive growth of the education system has been the subject of much historical research but it is one characterised by a number of different perspectives. Early historiography assumed that gradual state involvement in the education of its citizens marked a progressive advance towards the modern age. From this perspective, the first Parliamentary grant which gave £20,000 to two voluntary education societies in 1833, led inexorably to the 1870 Education Act which set up Board Schools, the 1880 Education Act which made schooling compulsory, the 1891 Education Act which gave parents the right to demand a free education for their children and ultimately the 1902 Education Act which supported the expansion of secondary education. Step by slow educational step, the foundations of the English educational system was laid. State intervention, by its very nature, was thought to be 'a good thing'.

This interpretation underwent serious revision when historians began to criticise the assumption that the history of education was the history of progress. Instead, the concept of social control was employed to explain the development of state education. Social control theorists believe that the middle-class providers of education attempted to impose a monolithic educational system on to the working-class recipients. Schooling, it was alleged, inculcated correct moral values, instilled a respect for authority and taught good time-keeping to children in preparation for their role as working-class adults. More recently, historians have begun to favour a subtler approach than that espoused by social control theorists. Educational systems, it is argued, are both progressive in that they act as a focus for change as well as reactionary in that the values of the dominant class are learned and reinforced. This interpretation suggests that the opportunities given to working-class children were framed within the context of an under-financed education system.

All of these interpretations share a common perspective in that they emphasise the question of class at the expense of gender. New interpretations have been put forward by feminist historians which reveal the importance of gender in education. Gender adds a new perspective to the previous historiography by demonstrating that the schooling for girls and boys was quite different. Gender, however, cannot be examined in isolation. This chapter will argue that the educational developments of the nineteenth century were defined by both gender and class and will examine part of the gender equation by focussing on the education of girls. First of all the education of the working-class girl will be considered, this will be followed by a discussion of the education of the middle-class girl and finally an examination of education for women.

1 The Education of Working-class Girls

Between 1800 and 1914 education was provided for the working-class girl through three main channels: institutional schools, religious schools and private schools. It was an informal system which relied upon charitable donations, state finance or private fees. After 1870, Board Schools replaced many of these disparate educational establishments to provide state education for working-class children. Feminist historians differ in their interpretation of the development and nature of working-class girls' education. Some argue that there was little or no gender distinction between working-class girls and boys at the beginning of the nineteenth century as both sexes were offered a similar meagre educational diet. Others disagree, arguing that the curriculum was different for girls and boys in all types of schools. All admit, however, that gender divisions were fundamental after 1870 when newly built Board Schools offered a different curriculum to girls and boys. The evidence which will be offered below should allow you to reach your own conclusions.

a) Institutional Education

Changes in working-class education often went hand in hand with other changes such as factory and poor law reform. Indeed, the two main providers of institutional education in the early nineteenth century were the factory and the workhouse. For children of the working class, education in these places was all too depressingly similar, irrespective of their sex. From 1833 cotton manufacturers were legally bound to provide half-time schooling for the children who worked in their factory. Factory schools were of varied quality but all taught reading, writing and arithmetic (commonly referred to as the three R's) within a gendered framework. Even forward thinking philanthropic mill owners adopted systems which differentiated between boys and girls: boys at Samuel Greg's school at Styal, near Manchester, were taught arithmetic, writing and religion but girls were taught sewing and 'other domestic avocations'. Similarly, in Strutt's mill at Belper girls were taught to knit and sew for about half the schooling time whereas boys concentrated on the more serious subjects of reading and writing. There were exceptions such as Robert Owen's school, opened in 1816 at New Lanark, which marked a decisive break from the dominance of the three R's and the rigid discipline found in the majority of factory schools. Influenced by progressive educational theory, Owen stressed the individuality and distinctiveness of each child and aimed to produce 'fully formed men and women, physically and mentally, who would always think and act consistently and rationally'. Owen offered a wider curriculum than most factory schools by including geography, history, nature study, dancing, singing and drill in the curriculum of all pupils. Pupils were amused with games and stories suited to their ability and taught in large, well-decorated rooms full with paintings and maps. Girls and boys were dressed in the same uniform, a toga-like white garment, and taught in the same classroom, thus seemingly breaking down gender divisions still further. However, despite Owen's progressive educational theories, only girl pupils had to learn to sew in his schools.

Workhouse schools were significantly inferior to factory schools. The 1834 Poor Law Amendment Act had created schools within workhouses for children of pauper parents. The education offered was equally limiting for both sexes but it was different so that girls were trained for domestic service and boys for labouring jobs. Indeed, girls spent more time as seamstresses, laundresses and cleaners than in learning to read, justified because girls were being trained for a future job.

b) Religious Schools

The majority of working-class children received their education part time in schools set up to inculcate religious principles in the pupils. Two of the most important charitable institutions set up by religious bodies were the Sunday schools and monitorial schools but they offered a similarly gendered curriculum, little different from that provided by the factory and the workhouse.

Sunday schools, popularised by Robert Raikes in the late eighteenth century, were financed by a number of religious denominations such as the Anglicans, Wesleyans and Quakers. Historians who subscribe to the social control theory of education suggest that Sunday schools attempted to impose a middle-class ethos on to the working class and tried to teach the poor to accept their station in life. All of these schools taught working-class children on Sundays so that it did not interrupt paid work. They aimed to teach no more than basic literacy and religion, therefore most pupils, both boys and girls, were taught only to read the Bible. Sunday schools rarely taught writing both because it was perceived as a secular rather than a religious activity and because a fully literate working-class adult might threaten the livelihood of the lower-middle-class clerical worker.

Sunday schools were especially important for girls in the first half of the nineteenth century because they often offered them their only educational opportunity. In 1800 literacy rates for women, based on their ability to sign the marriage register, were about 33 per cent but by 1861 almost two and a half million children, mostly girls, were enrolled in a Sunday school. The majority of girls did not attend day schools because parents preferred to keep their daughters at home to help with household duties or else to send them out to work. Nevertheless, the opportunities proposed were even more limited for girls than for boys because Sunday schools operated a hidden curriculum which reinforced subordination. Separate seating arrangements for girls and boys reinforced sexual difference, whereas religious texts consolidated a message of female inferiority.

Full-time education was provided by two rival religious groups: the Anglican National Society and the Nonconformist British and Foreign Schools Society. Before the 1870 Education Act these two societies delivered most of the voluntary education for the working class. Both societies used the monitorial system whereby teachers, using monitors as assistants, were able to instruct hundreds of boys and girls at the same time. Monitorial schools, as they became known, allegedly targeted boys rather than girls: for instance, the flagship schools of each society had double the number of boys as girls enrolled. There was, however, a regional difference in that girls were in a minority in urban schools but there were an almost equal number of girls and boys in rural communities. The curriculum, both overt and hidden, was however gendered. One historian has noted that sexual divisions between girls and boys were formalised in monitorial schools, indicated by the separate entrances, separate classes and separate time-tables.

Initially, the aim of the voluntary societies was to teach the three Rs but by the 1830s the emphasis on literacy was inadequate. Social unrest combined with economic and industrial change prompted a reappraisal of the education system being provided. Education, it was believed, furnished the means to civilise the working class by cultivating middle-class values at school and educating children for future employment. Middle-class values, however, were different for boys than for girls: boys were taught to be industrious and punctual whereas girls were expected to be chaste and obedient. In 1841 the aim of the National Society was to 'teach the young women to be sober, to love their husbands, to love their children, to be discreet, chaste, keepers at home, obedient to their husbands that the word of God be not blasphemed'. Girls, expected to become wives and mothers or domestic servants, had their domestic role reinforced. Accordingly, girls were taught cookery, sewing and housekeeping in preparation for their future lives as shown by this extract from the National Society in 1861 which had 'no desire to make girls little Newtons, little Captain Cooks, little Livingstones, little Mozarts and Handels ... will ever take us too low for keeping in sight the object of teaching them to make and mend shirts, to make and mend pinafores, and darn stockings and socks'. At Sandbach a specially constructed wash-house and kitchen was built for the girl pupils to wash the linen of the church, the teachers and themselves and to learn how to cook. However, the sophisticated and high-tech wash-house and kitchen of Sandbach was far removed from the homes of most working-class people so one Norwich school bought two small houses where girls could feel more 'at home' learning domestic skills.

Sometimes this domestic curriculum was rarely taught because parental objection, combined with limited resources, meant it could not be offered. Parents disliked practical subjects, preferring their children to be educated rather than trained; 'shan't be turned into scrubs' one parent commented. Many refused to send their children to schools which emphasised menial tasks and appeared to have little desire to subscribe to the domestication of working-class girls. In addition, providing suitable materials was often prohibitively expensive. To overcome this, a few schools used girl pupils to clean the school, help out at the local parsonage or wash the laundry of the school mistress - and justified it as training in domestic skills. Inspectors suggested that girls learn some domestic skills through lessons in arithmetic, writing and chemistry so that adding up shopping bills and writing on topics such as how to boil a leg of mutton were recommended as ways to teach domestic skills. Chemistry lessons were similarly functional in teaching domestic skills: one inspector suggested that girls might learn basic chemistry by watching cookery demonstrations.

The majority of schools, unable to afford the materials for cooking lessons, gave priority to needlework. It was cheap to learn to sew and could be used to support the teaching of religion when the girls sewed samplers bearing messages such as 'God is Love'. Needles, thread and scissors were inexpensive tools compared with the cost of cooking utensils but, even so, girls learned to sew on paper before being allowed to use cloth. Once competent, girls learnt to sew goods which were later sold to the public: in 1862 the Bayswater National School earned over £36 from selling 326 articles made by the girls of the school. Others relied on their school committees to supply them with articles such as handkerchiefs and towels to be hemmed by the girls, but sometimes the girls made clothes for themselves which they later bought at cost price. Needlework took up between three to five half-days per week which fitted well with the National Society's ethos which suggested in 1833 that 'In a well managed school for girls, half the day may be given to needlework, or knitting, and the other half will suffice for acquiring a knowledge of reading, writing and summing, besides a more familiar acquaintance with the most important religious truths'.

However, needlework, like cookery, was not taught in all schools because there was no one to teach it. For example, if a school employed all male teachers then girls were taught the same subjects as the boys. Fears that girls were not being taught needlework provoked the government to take remedial action and in 1846 needlework was made a compulsory subject for girls who intended to become teachers, prompting one inspector to remark that the instruction of girl children 'is not so much in reading, writing and arithmetic, as in reading, writing and needlework'. The Revised Code of 1862 consolidated the domestication of girl pupils for under this system, which lasted from 1862 until 1890, grants were paid partly on attendance and partly on exam results. Schools claimed four shillings for each pupil who attended school regularly and were given further grants if pupils passed certain subjects. Thus when the Revised Code made needlework obligatory for all girl pupils, grant payment was withheld if girls were not taught needlework. This prompted Rochdale Parochial school to exclude girl pupils completely because they feared a reduction in school grant.

Not all monitorial schools offered such a gendered, or indeed such a religiously defined, curriculum. In 1854 the feminist and Nonconformist Barbara Bodichon founded a monitorial school in London in line with her radical ideas on sexual equality. This school provided a secular education for children of all social classes and nationalities and boys and girls were taught together and offered the same wide range of subjects. Visits to museums, picture galleries and libraries supplemented the curriculum for both boys and girls. A former pupil wrote 'The chief thing that I remember ... was the gentle influence which pervaded the school, and the capital order which was obtained without corporal punishment. ... There was a feeling, too, of cheerful alacrity and pleasure in the work, both on the part of the teachers and pupils, and the lessons were so varied that they never became wearisome.' This shortlived experiment - the school only lasted three years - was virtually unique and drew large-scale criticism from the clergy who objected to the undenominational nature of the school.

c) Dame Schools

Given the inadequacy of charitable schooling, it is perhaps not surprising that many working-class parents chose to send their children to dame schools. These schools were sometimes run by discharged soldiers but they were usually managed by women who at best taught basic literacy to young children for a small fee. Dame schools have suffered from a great deal of adverse criticism as they were perceived to be little more than child-minding establishments where untrained, semi-literate teachers misinformed their young pupils. The Secretary of State for Education, Kay-Shuttleworth quoted a report of 1834-5 which stated:

1 The greater part of them are kept by females, but some by old men, whose only qualification for this employment seems to be their unfitness for every other. Many of these teachers are engaged at the same time in some other employment, such as shopkeeping, 5 sewing, washing etc.

However, criticism of dame schools has largely been based on two pieces of government evidence: HMI Reports and the Newcastle Commission Report of 1861, the authors of which favoured the charity school system. Recent interpretations suggest that dame schools were more efficient than previously supposed. Certainly, dame schools were popular with working-class parents who chose to pay more for their children to attend a dame school than for the allegedly superior church schools. Working-class parents preferred dame schools to those founded and managed by the middle class for a number of reasons. Dame schools were managed by working-class women so there was little danger that middle class values were imposed on working class children. In addition, they fitted comfortably into the working life style, they were located nearby, were much smaller than those managed by charities, had a homely atmosphere, were perceived to be more tolerant, less rule-bound and rigid, less obsessed with time-keeping and attendance and less disciplinarian than the monitorial schools. It was also believed that pupils learned to read more quickly in the smaller dame schools than they did in the monitorial schools which held much larger numbers of pupils. Indeed, some historians have argued that neither girls nor boys were inculcated with middle-class gendered values in dame schools because they were owned and controlled by the working class. However, it is hard to generalise about dame schools because their quality varied tremendously and detailed evidence is lacking but, according to the

A dame school

evidence collected to date, many taught the gender-specific skills of needlework to girls only.

d) Effects of the 1870 Education Act

The period from 1870 to 1914 saw the construction of a state education system which consolidated gender divisions. The 1870 Education Act encouraged the newly formed School Boards to build schools in areas not covered by charitable bodies, but in 1902 Local Education Authorities replaced the School Board system and were empowered to develop secondary education. Fears that Britain was in moral decline prompted educationalists and governments to attempt to reinforce family ties. Teaching girls domestic skills was thought to be a cure for the demise of family values and the potential disintegration of the nation and society. In 1878 domestic science was made a compulsory subject in the Board Schools. Topics included food and its preparation, how to look after a house, wash clothes and take care of a budget. However, as with the charity schools, lack of resources often hindered the implementation of the domestic science curriculum: one inspector in the north of England reported a lesson on roasting meat in which a solitary chop was prepared and cooked by 18 girls! At the same time there was a move to make science more relevant to girl pupils, so a growing emphasis was placed on domestic science as opposed to the pure sciences. Such innovation led to great resistance, particularly by female science teachers who feared their hard-won gains might be eroded by placing science so firmly in the domestic sphere.

Of course, the emphasis on domesticity meant that various other important subjects were ignored. Arithmetic, for example, was given a low priority in girls' schools so, not surprisingly, girls did less well. One can conclude that the educational change of the nineteenth century affected girl pupils less than it did their male counterparts. The social upshot of the decision to domesticate working-class girls was to reinforce their familial role, keep them economically dependent and make it difficult for them to seek well-paid jobs.

2 The Education of the Middle- and Upper-class Girl

a) Middle and Upper-class Education

While middle- and upper-class education differed profoundly from that of the working class, it was similar in one important respect: girls of all social classes were destined to get married and raise a family. Consequently, it was a time when educational provision for middle- and upper-class English girls was generally of poor quality. The majority of these girls did not attend school but were taught at home by their mothers, fathers and other relatives. Education was on an *ad hoc* basis and depended on who was available to teach. Girls from wealthy families enjoyed a more systematic approach as tutors and governesses were engaged to teach a range of subjects and other accomplishments. However, the quality of home tuition, whether given by relatives or paid teachers, varied considerably. Dorothea Beale was educated by a rapid succession of inadequate governesses who taught her and her sisters very little. She wrote in her autobiography that 'My mother advertised and hundreds of answers were sent. She began by eliminating all those in which bad spelling occurred. ... I can remember only one really clever and competent teacher'. In direct contrast, many Nonconformist families educated their daughters in the same way as their sons so that the quality of home education for girls was higher. The Unitarian, Florence Nightingale, for example, was taught classics, modern languages, history and philosophy by her father. In addition, Nonconformist young women enjoyed a social and political education denied to their peers. Elizabeth Cadbury, daughter of a Birmingham Quaker family, was brought up by parents committed to the abolition of slavery as well as temperance, educational and prison reform. However, whatever the social and religious background of the family, home tuition had one major aim: women were expected to catch a husband rather than find a paid job.

Sometimes the daughters of upper-class wealthy parents were privately educated at boarding schools which held a small number of selective pupils. The more expensive schools were in London and the fashionable towns of Brighton and Bath and charged fees of, on average, £140 a year but sometimes as high as £500. High fees, however, did not match intellectual attainment. One Brighton school which drew from the daughters of the landed gentry and aristocracy had a curriculum based on deportment and drawing. One of its pupils, who later became a leading feminist had this to say of it:

1 The din of our large double schoolrooms was something frightful. Sitting in either of them, four pianos might be heard going at once in rooms above and around us, while at numerous tables scattered about the rooms there were girls reading aloud to the governesses.
5 ...
  Nobody dreamt that any one of us could in later life be more or less than an 'Ornament to Society'. That a pupil in that school could ever become an artist or an authoress, would have been led upon as a deplorable dereliction. Everything was taught us in the
10 inverse ratio of its true importance. At the bottom of the scales were Morals and Religion, and at the top were Music and Dancing. ... The waste of money involved in all this, the piles of useless music and songs never to be sung, for which our parents had to pay, and the loss of priceless time for ourselves, were truly
15 deplorable. ...

Next to music in importance in our curriculum came dancing ...
we had learned not only all the dances in use in England in that
anti-polka epoch, but almost every national dance in Europe, the
Minuet, the Gavotte, the Cachucha, the Bolero, the Mazurka and
20 the Tarantella. ...

I know as much as any girl in our school, and since it is the best
school in England, I must know all that it can ever be necessary for
a lady to know.

Less wealthy middle-class parents sent their daughters to day schools or
cheaper, less fashionable, boarding schools which were even more
inferior than the high fee paying boarding schools. In some boarding
schools, in mid nineteenth-century England, girls endured humiliating
punishments. At one school young girls were punished for telling lies by
being forced to stand in a corner of the schoolroom wearing a long black
gown with a piece of red cloth cut in the shape of a tongue with the
words LIAR on it. Whether this treatment was aimed to instil honesty or
was merely an aid to the smooth running of the school is hard to judge.

At the end of a more or less expensive education, 'young ladies' were
able to play a few tunes on the piano, to sing, to dance the Minuet, to
draw a simple sketch, to sew a delicate sampler and sometimes to speak a
little French. These accomplishments helped them achieve the
Victorian ideal of the perfect educated woman: a decorative, poised and
empty-headed companion for a future husband. The low academic
standard of such schools prompted one feminist to remark that girls
were taught the three S's rather than the three R's: singing, sewing and
simpering. Indeed, the state of girls' education was summed up by the
Taunton Commission of 1868: 'We find, as a rule, a very small amount
of professional skill, an inferior set of school books, a vast deal of dry,
uninteresting task work, rules put into the memory with no explanation
of their principles, no system of examination worthy of the name.' Even
in Scotland, with a history of co-educational schools, girls were offered a
markedly different curriculum from the boys. Whereas most boys
learned Latin, few girls did so. As in English schools, the Scottish system
emphasised domestic skills rather than intellectual ones. On the other
hand, schools managed by Unitarians were significantly different. In
Liverpool, girls at Rachel Martineau's school enjoyed a similar
curriculum as boys and many other Nonconformist schools emphasised
academic rather than domestic achievement. Nonetheless, despite
regional and religious differences, education was curiously detached
from academic excellence.

b) Changes in the Education of Middle- and Upper-class Girls

Not surprisingly, feminists attempted to refashion girls' education into a
more positive approach. In contrast to the changes in working-class

girls' education which were imposed from above, the impetus for middle- and upper-class educational reform originated in pressure from below. Middle- and upper-class women concerned about the inadequacy of girls' education worked hard to improve it. Two, somewhat contradictory, arguments were put forward in support of improved educational opportunities for girls from this social class. On the one hand, it was argued that better education would make women better wives and mothers. Husbands wanted wives who could discuss current affairs and engage in intelligent conversation rather than empty-headed playthings. Well educated women, it was alleged, made superior mothers because they were better placed to teach their children. On the other hand, others believed that higher educational standards improved job prospects. Concern was expressed that middle-class spinsters, many of whom needed to earn a living, were inadequately prepared for the world of work.

Opponents of educational reform focussed on the damage such education might bring upon women, their families and wider society. It was feared that education damaged women's reproductive ability and created mannish women who decried marriage - a fear confirmed when only a quarter of Oxford and Cambridge graduates married. Educated women would allegedly compete with middle-class men for professional jobs and thus upset the social order. As a consequence of improved educational opportunities for women the birth rate would decline, relationships between the sexes would break down, family life would be undermined and societal values would be threatened. In 1868, one antifeminist, Sarah Sewell who was strongly opposed to women's education wrote:

1   The education of girls need not be of the same extended, classical, and commercial character as that of boys; they want more an education of the heart and feelings, and especially of firm, fixed, moral principles. They should be made conversant with history,
5   geography, figures, the poets, and general literature, with a sure groundwork of religion and obedience. The profoundly educated women rarely make good wives and mothers. The pride of knowledge does not amalgamate well with the everyday matter-of-fact rearing of children, and women who have stored their minds
10 with Latin and Greek seldom have much knowledge of pies and puddings, nor do they enjoy the hard and uninteresting work of attending to the wants of little children; and those women, poor things, who have lost their most attractive charm of womanliness, and are seen on the public platforms, usurping the exclusive duties
15 of men, are seldom seen in their nurseries; though they may become notorious themselves, their children rarely do them credit, and the energy they throw away on the equalising bubble, would be much better expended in a more womanly and motherly manner,

in looking after their husbands' comforts, the training of their
20 children, and the good of the household at large.

In spite of such opposition the campaigns for educational reform
continued to grow. In particular, a new crop of schools was established
in the mid nineteenth century which allegedly provided a welcome
antidote to the traditional girls' schools. They were run by trustees on a
professional basis and aimed to offer an academic education to
middle-class girls. Nonetheless these schools adopted a cautious
approach to change and provide an interesting contradiction in
educational reform. There was a desire to improve the academic rigour
and content of girls' education but this progress was contained within
the existing, narrow framework of femininity. On the one hand, girls
were intellectually challenged yet still expected to behave in a ladylike
manner. Furthermore, these new girls' schools only educated a minority
of girls as 70 per cent remained at the old private schools in the latter
part of the nineteenth century.

One historian has categorised these new schools in two ways: day
high schools and the newer boarding schools.The North London
Collegiate School, founded by Frances Mary Buss in 1850, was seen
to be the role model for the rest of the girls' high schools. It catered
largely for the daughters of the lower middle class and accepted girls
of all religious denominations. Pupils at the North London Collegiate
School learned a double message of independence mixed with
femininity. On the one hand, the North London Collegiate School
offered a broader curriculum than the established girls' schools and
placed high priority on passing the local examinations of Oxford and
Cambridge (the contemporary equivalent of GCSE's). Pupils were
also encouraged to proceed to higher education or to join the Civil
Service. On the other hand the North London Collegiate stressed
femininity: for example, girls had to remain gloved at all times in the
street and were not allowed to walk more than three in a row. Formal
lessons were held in the mornings only to allow girls to learn
accomplishments in the afternoons or return home to help their
mothers. A sewing club called the Dorcas Society was also established
which encouraged girls to sew clothing which was later distributed to
the poor - a task deemed suitable for women destined to be part of
the socially conscious middle class. These features of the North
London Collegiate were adopted by a number of other girls' schools
established at that time. In 1869 the Endowed Schools Act provided
the money to found grammar schools such as the Manchester High
School for girls and in 1872 the Girls' Public Day School Trust
(GPDST) was launched which in turn established 38 nondenominational schools. As with the North London Collegiate, the GPDST
championed a wider curriculum of science, economics and mathematics for girls but also emphasised their role as wives and mothers.

At the same time, a few exclusive boarding schools were also opened for the daughters of the more privileged. In 1854 Cheltenham Ladies' College was established but it was not until Dorothea Beale arrived as Principal that the school attained national fame. When Dorothea Beale first arrived pupil numbers had dropped significantly. Little by little, she transformed the school into one of the most prestigious in England but it was not an easy task. Only very gradually were Mathematics, Science, Latin and Greek introduced and new teaching methods adopted because of the resistance of some parents. One father who took his daughters away from the school said 'My dear lady, if my daughters were going to be bankers, it would be very well to teach arithmetic as you do, but there is no need'. Slowly, but systematically, Beale persuaded parents that her educational philosophy was becoming for upper-class girls. High academic standards were expected and exam marks were read out and commented upon in front of the whole class as an incentive to work hard.

Cheltenham Ladies' College never was, and Dorothea Beale never meant it to be, a school which favoured social equality. It remained highly exclusive. High fees and selection procedures debarred the majority of girls in Cheltenham. Only the daughters of independent gentlemen or professionals were accepted, for the school refused to admit any girl who was in a 'lower' class of society. Daughters of tradespeople were refused admittance even when they could afford the fees. Nevertheless, Cheltenham Ladies' College provided inspiration to others as it proved that girls could reach and maintain high educational standards. And so, in 1877, St Leonards in Scotland, in 1885 Roedean near Brighton, in 1896 Wycombe Abbey near London were founded from the exemplar of Cheltenham.

3 Further and Higher Education

a) Working-class Women

The vast majority of working-class women were not educated beyond elementary school level but some studied part time in the evenings, a few became pupil teachers and a tiny minority obtained a scholarship to higher education. However, as with elementary schooling, women's higher education was located firmly within a class and gendered context.

Most working-class women needed to earn a living and so tended to enrol as part-time students in Mechanics' Institutes or Working Men's Colleges if they wished to extend their education. Mechanics Institutes were founded in the 1820s to educate working-class men but a few institutions reluctantly offered classes to women. Even so, women remained a small minority, rarely gained full membership, paid a lower subscription rate, were offered fewer facilities and were often not allowed to use the common room. Moreover, women were taught separately from men and were offered a limited curriculum based on class and gender stereotypes. For example, working-class women were taught the three R's, plain sewing and a little general knowledge, whereas male students were offered a broader range of subjects such as history, geography and classics.

Working men's colleges were founded in the 1850s as an alternative to Mechanics' Institutes but these served women just as badly. As with the Mechanics' Institutes, women were presented with a curriculum thought to equip them for their future domestic role as wives and mothers. In Halifax, for example, men were able to study a range of subjects from algebra, chemistry, geography, history, French and theology whereas women were only allowed to study reading, writing, arithmetic, and of course sewing and cookery. On the other hand, the London Working Men's College concentrated on the ladylike accomplishments of drawing, singing and botany rather than basic domestic skills because it attracted a more upwardly mobile female clientele.

Criticisms were made of the narrow curriculum in the working men's colleges but the managers of these institutions were impervious to change. As a consequence, women set up one alternative institution which offered a broader and less gender-stereotyped curriculum. The Working Women's College which opened in Bloomsbury in 1864 viewed women as prospective intellectuals rather than wives and mothers, so provided courses in Anglo-Saxon, geometry, logic, physiology, political economy and zoology for its female scholars. However, no other women's college was founded and even the Working Women's College was unable to be financially viable so ten years later, after an acrimonious debate, it opened its doors to men.

Clever and highly motivated working-class women also gained an education through teacher training. In 1846 Kay-Shuttleworth initiated a scheme whereby grants were given to the best-equipped elementary schools to train teachers. At the age of 13 the most promising pupils were apprenticed to the headmaster for five years (which created misgivings as to the effectiveness of entrusting academic education to schools) to learn how to teach. Each year the pupil-teacher sat an exam based on a prescribed syllabus which, after the introduction of the Revised Code, was narrow in focus. Female pupil-teachers were not expected to reach the same standard as male pupil-teachers in arithmetic but were expected to be proficient in needlework. By the 1880s the pupil-teacher system was being heavily criticised for its lack of intellectual rigour but it continued until 1902 when secondary school education replaced pupil apprenticeship.

The pupil-teacher scheme was accompanied by developments in teacher training colleges. At the age of 18 pupil-teachers could sit for a competitive examination which enabled them to attend a training college for up to three years. Successful pupil teachers were thus able to augment their school experience with a year at college, helped by a system of grants. In 1842 the first women's college was founded at Whitelands but this, like the colleges which followed, used trainee students as domestic helps. This domestic work was justified because students were expected to teach these skills in elementary schools but the emphasis on domesticity owed as much to economic factors as educational ones: using trainee teachers as domestics cut the cost of managing the Training College quite considerably.

b) Middle-class Women

At the beginning of the nineteenth century, women were denied access to full-time higher education as universities were closed to them. By 1900 this had changed. There were three main strands to higher education for middle-class women: the colleges founded specifically for women, the University Extension classes and the universities themselves.

The struggle for women's education was hard fought because it challenged the basis on which society was founded. As one historian has noted, the pioneers of higher education had 'to fight for a new ideal of middle-class femininity, the ideal of the new woman who could study the same subjects as men and enter paid, professional employment'. The women who enrolled in these various institutions were therefore caught in the crossfire of educational change for they suffered from two contradictory expectations. On the one hand they were expected to meet exacting academic standards, while on the other hand they were expected to conform to feminine stereotypes.

One of the first triumphs for middle-class women who wanted to continue their education was the foundation of new London colleges set up specifically for women. In 1848, the Anglican, Queens College was founded, by men, to raise the academic status of governesses and to provide a training centre for women engaged in social work. A quite different college, Bedford, was opened for women in 1849 by a wealthy Unitarian woman. Unlike Queens' it was nondenominational and governed by women. Both Queens' and Bedford really offered secondary rather than higher education but Bedford College eventually reached university status whereas Queens became a selective girls' secondary school. Nevertheless many of the leading feminists of the day attended either Queens or Bedford college. Barbara Bodichon, Dorothea Beale, Frances Buss, Bessie Rayner Parkes, Sophia Jex Blake, women who will be mentioned in subsequent chapters, all gained their education at one of these colleges.

Women also gained access to higher education via University Extension classes. The University Extension movement began in 1867 when a male Cambridge don delivered a course of lectures in a few major cities. Large numbers of women attended these lectures which prompted sympathetic male lecturers to offer extension classes to women who wished to prolong their education.

Apparently, the large numbers of women present at University extension classes shaped the way in which classes were taught. Lecturers, aware that most of their audience lacked note taking skills, printed the main points of their talk to help their female audience follow the lecture. Women were also encouraged to read academic texts and write essays which were marked by university staff. University Extension classes provided many women with their only entrance to academia but some feminists were critical of the movement because they feared that extension classes might become a substitute for university education.

The hardest educational struggle for women was to win acceptance at traditional universities. These universities were a male preserve which provided a professional education for lawyers, doctors, the clergy and secondary teachers, all professions closed to women. In 1828, London University became the first English university to open up its scholarly doors to women when they were permitted to join lectures at King's and University College. Many years later, in 1869, Emily Davies helped to found a women's college at Hitchin which later became Girton College, Cambridge. Davies held to what she termed 'A Grand Principle' that women should study the same subjects as men and be expected to pass similar exams. Education, Davies believed, must never be watered down to accommodate women. On the contrary, she was uncompromising in ensuring that women met the same exacting intellectual standards as men and refused to support a differentiated curriculum for women. In contrast, Newnham College, Cambridge, founded just after Girton, devised special courses for its undergraduates. At Newnham students were encouraged to study the traditional female subjects of English language and history and not compete on the same terms as men. Ten years later, in 1879, Somerville College and Lady Margaret Hall were founded in Oxford, swiftly followed by provincial colleges throughout England and Scotland. Although women were permitted to study at Oxbridge they were disbarred from receiving degrees: Cambridge University did not award degrees to women until 1947.

Whether they attended university at Oxford, Cambridge or London, all female university students shared much in common in that they were expected to conform to a feminine stereotype. Fearing criticism that they might become de-sexed, female students were expected to dress demurely and behave in a 'ladylike' manner at all times. Smoking was strictly prohibited. Women's physical freedom was severely restricted as they were chaperoned in lectures and at all social occasions. Female students at Manchester University were not allowed to use the library in person because as one student stated 'it would have been deemed the height of impropriety to enter the library and demand a book in the hardened manner now usual. No, we had to 'fill up a voucher' and a dear little maid of all work, aged about 13 went to the library with it'. Perhaps more importantly, women students and indeed staff at all universities were discouraged from participating in political events in case it reflected badly on the college they attended. At Oxford, for instance, the majority of students and staff supported votes for women but, when a suffrage meeting was held at Somerville, the Secretary to the Council of the College resigned and her husband withdrew his subscription, so great was the fear of public disapproval.

The growth of women's education may have been dramatic in the nineteenth century but educational opportunities were different for middle-class and working-class women. Indeed, by the end of the century education had polarised class differences because women were offered different access to education which, in turn, led ultimately to unequal job opportunities. Education may have facilitated the entry of middle-class women into alternative employment but it reinforced working-class women's domestic role by limiting their educational choice.

Making notes on *'The Gendering of Education'*

The simplest way to take notes for this chapter would be to follow the headings used in the text before examining each section in greater detail. Before you do this, try to keep the first paragraph of this chapter in mind. To what extent were educational developments humanitarian? To what extent were working-class educational improvements about social control? How gendered was education for girls? Using this analytical framework should enable you to take more focussed notes on, for example, religious education rather than regurgitating the facts.

Source-based questions on *'The Gendering of Education'*

1 The Aims of the National Society
Read the source extracts on page 31. Answer the following questions.
a) What are the explicit aims of the National Society? (3 marks)
b) How might an historian who favoured i) an humanitarian
    perspective ii) a social control perspective iii) a gendered perspective
    interpret these extracts? (9 marks)
c) Compare these aims with those of Bodichon's school. (4 marks)

2 A Fashionable School
Read the extracts from Frances Power Cobbe on pages 36 and 37. Answer the following questions.
a) According to the school, what were the necessary accomplishments for a lady to learn? (2 marks)
b) How valid was Power Cobbe's criticism of them?

3 Opposition to Women's Education

Read the extract from Sarah Sewell on pages 38 and 39. Answer the following questions.

a) What does Sewell mean by 'though they may become notorious themselves, their children rarely do them credit'. (2 marks)

b) How justifiable is Sewell's criticisms of women's education? (4 marks)

c) Compare Frances Power Cobbe's view of education with Sewell's. (5 marks)

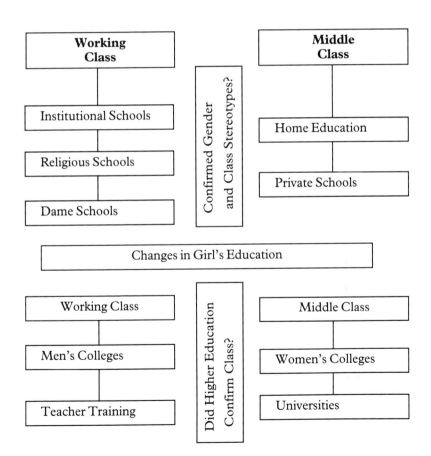

Summary - The Gendering of Education

4 A Dame School

Look at the engraving on page 35. Answer the following questions.

a)   How gendered was the curriculum of this dame school?
     (3 marks)
b)   How does this dame school compare to the ones described by
     Kay-Shuttleworth? (4 marks)
c)   How useful do you think this engraving is to an historian studying
     the educational effectiveness of dame schools? (4 marks)

CHAPTER 4

Women and Work

Histories of women's work, to a greater extent than histories of domesticity and education, reflect the growth of women's history very broadly. Initially, historians concentrated on discovering evidence about the participation of women in industrialisation. These studies added to our knowledge and demonstrated the enormous contribution made by women to the wealth of the nation but tended to be both descriptive and adulatory. More recent scholarship suggests the need for a theoretical framework with which to understand industrial transformation. Socialist historians used the category of 'class' to explain the process of industrialisation but they tended to ignore women's role in the world of work. Feminist historians added the category of 'gender' to analyse the difference between men's and women's work. They recognised that women experienced industrialisation in quite distinct ways from men. Work, for instance, was sexually segregated. Even more so than men's work, women's work was usually low paid, monotonous, unskilled, of low status, casual and lacking in career prospects. Many jobs were often domestically based thus reinforcing women's roles as wife and mother. Gender distinctions, just as much as class ones, were therefore seen to affect the development of industrialisation. Nonetheless, class remained important as the working patterns of the working-class and middle-class women remained distinctive.

1 Working-class Women and Work

a) Effects of Industrialisation

The period covered by this book is one in which Britain consolidated her industrial base. By 1850 the transformation from an agricultural to an industrial nation was more or less complete. There used to be two contrasting views on the effect of this industrialisation on women. Optimists suggested that industrialisation provided greater employment prospects which led, in turn, to women's emancipation. Factory work, for example, was believed to be less physically demanding, cleaner, more congenial and better paid than work in the pre-industrial economy. Cotton workers enjoyed a degree of economic independence and autonomy unknown to their pre-industrial colleagues. This view was challenged by historians who offered a more pessimistic interpretation. They argued that far from liberating women, industrialisation increased exploitation and led to longer hours, lower wages and a more rigid sexual division of labour, all of which consolidated women's economically inferior position. New technology was not thought to provide women with greater job opportunities as they were not employed in the high prestige trades of heavy engineering, transport, the scientific trades and shipbuilding, which were categorised as men's work. On the contrary, women were concentrated in the textile trades and the domestic service industry at wages far below men's. The following extract from the 1841 census, which covered England and Wales, appears to confirm the pessimistic interpretation because it demonstrates some of the occupations traditionally performed by women, as well as showing the absence of women in certain skilled work:

	over 20	under 20
Baker	3,144	79
Bonnet maker	3,331	976
Boot and shoe maker	8,611	1,953
Brick layer	106	-
Butcher	1,047	26
Charwoman	18,019	265
Coal labourer	184	187
Cotton worker	65,839	49,586
Domestic servant	447,606	264,887
Engine and machine maker	45	8
Farmer	13,398	-
Farm labourer	26,815	8,447
Gun maker	67	15
Laundry worker	43,497	1,522
Lodging house owner	6,073	33
Mason	146	4
Publican	5,574	3

However, census returns have been shown by historians to seriously underrecord women's work by sometimes as much as a third, so they must be used with care. Despite this weakness, census returns do provide the historian with an overview of some of the work performed by women. In many ways, the census extract given above fits neatly into the pessimistic approach whereby women's traditional role is confirmed. Notwithstanding, historians now reject the polarisation of women's work into pessimistic and optimistic interpretations and favour an approach which stresses the complexities of the impact of industrialisation.

b) Home Working

Indeed, recent research indicates that women's work was not as affected by industrialisation as has sometimes been suggested. For example, cotton mills, the largest single employer of factory women, were generally limited to a small geographical area in the north-west of England. Many regions remained less affected by technological innovation. Apparently about 70 per cent of all the work force, even in

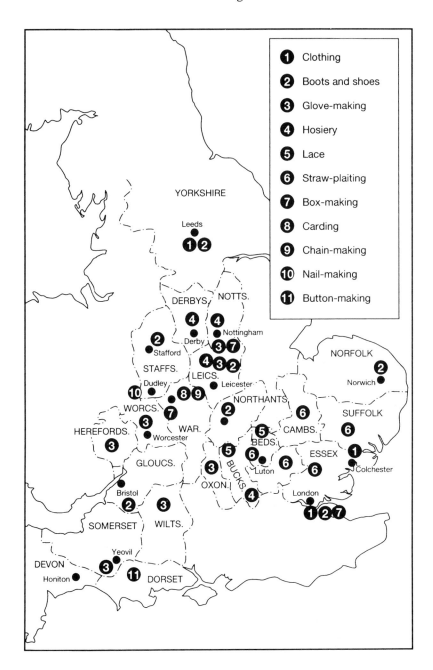

A map showing home-working areas in England

1861, were still employed in small non-industrialised workshops or as home-workers as the map on page 49 shows. Domestic workshops dominated the Midlands and London. At Cradley Heath, women of the Black Country made chains in sheds at the back of their houses, Nottingham was the centre of lace and hosiery, Northampton women made leather footwear, straw plaiting was popular in the South Midlands whereas in London laundry work, needlework and matchbox-making prevailed.

Home working continued well into the nineteenth century and only began to decline from the 1870s. It was favoured by employers and employees for quite different reasons. Married women (home working was predominantly a married woman's job) worked at home because their income supplemented the small wage of their husband and fitted in with domestic responsibilities. Lower-middle-class women, whose social position would have made work outside the home inconceivable, were able to take in home-work without challenging women's accepted vocation. Indeed, home-work accorded perfectly with women's traditional role as housewife and mother for work could be done at home in between housework, cooking and looking after the children. Older girls, not at school, were employed collecting the raw materials and returning finished work or else helping their mothers in small tasks. Nevertheless, it seems that homeworking was not the preferred choice of most women as it was only widespread in areas where there was little alternative work. Historians agree that homeworking occurred in places where working-class male wages were low, where seasonal work predominated, where there was little female employment or where there was a surplus of women. Home-workers, for example, were often the wives of poorly paid and casual agricultural or dock workers, or else they worked in places such as London or the Midlands which offered fewer employment opportunities for women, or in areas like Nottingham where there were considerably more females to males and women had to be financially self-supporting.

On the other hand, employers preferred to employ home-workers rather than set up a small factory because doing so maximised profits in a variety of ways. Employers were able to cut their overhead costs and save considerable sums of money on rent as home-workers not only worked at home but had to pay for the heating and lighting used in their work. They also saved on production costs. New technology was expensive so employers were reluctant to invest in heavy machinery unless it offered the prospect of significantly reduced costs of production. For instance, sewing machines which could be used at home provided an intermediate technology that was more economically viable and productive than larger equipment. Home-workers also offered a plentiful supply of cheap labour to employers who generally exploited their economic vulnerability mercilessly. The hours and conditions of home-workers were not protected by law, making them a desirable group to employ. Protective legislation (see page 58) had limited the hours of women and children in factories and had improved working conditions but there was nothing to stop home-workers being pressurised into working as many hours as necessary to complete the required level of production. Indeed, home-workers were a more malleable workforce than factory workers, many of whom joined trade unions to demand shorter hours and more money for the same work output. This working flexibility was extremely attractive to employers concerned about seasonal fluctuations in the demand for their goods. Full-time staff who were paid weekly may have drained an employer's profits but home-workers who were only engaged as and when they were needed were economically advantageous to employers who paid only for the work which was completed.

c) Domestic Service

Domestic service provides a good example of both changes and continuities in women's work during industrialisation. For example, between 1851 and 1871 the number of female servants grew twice as fast as the population as a whole but the nature of the work remained more or less the same. Domestic service continued to be the largest occupation for working-class women throughout the nineteenth century: in 1851 40 per cent of the employed female workforce were domestic servants, mostly under the age of 20. It is said that one in every three women in Victorian England was employed as a domestic servant at some time in their working lives. This increase took place, it is argued, for three main reasons. A dramatic growth in the middle class - between 1815 and 1871 the number of people who earned over £150 a year doubled - created a class which had enough spare money to pay for servants. These middle-class women expected to be freed from mundane domestic responsibilities, so many servants were employed to cook, clean and take care of the children. Secondly, as agricultural employment declined there were fewer job opportunities in the country areas. For rural women, domestic service remained the only viable, and respectable, occupation: two-thirds of domestic servants were said to be the daughters of rural labourers. Lastly, female servants were considerably cheaper than male servants so employers preferred them, indeed, the ratio of female servants to male was 100:13 according to the 1851 census.

The romanticised image of a domestic servant is of a young single woman, neatly dressed and wearing a crisply ironed, clean white apron and cap, scurrying soundlessly about in a large mansion. Domestic service, however, was rarely like this. A prosperous household employed many servants all of whom would perform different duties and had special skills. The kitchen maid, the parlour maid, the ladies' maid, the children's nurse, the cook, the housekeeper and the tweenie (maid of all work) were all part of a complex below-stairs regime. In large mansions there was an established hierarchy which ranged from the tweenie at the bottom through to the (male) butler who was at the top. Not everyone who employed domestic servants was wealthy enough to pay for a large staff. For the sole servant of an artisan family, called a 'slavey', it was much simpler: all of the household tasks from cleaning the grate to cooking the food, heaving buckets of coal weighing 30lbs, carrying children (prams were unknown until the late 1850s) and fetching heavy jugs of water were accomplished by one person. Nonetheless, whether domestic servants worked in a large mansion or a smaller home they were all engaged in the customary feminine role of cooking, cleaning and looking after the children.

Pay for servants differed, but as with most female jobs, remained low. Average wages in a large mansion ranged from £15-27 per annum for housemaids rising to between £40-£60 for housekeepers, which contrasted favourably with cotton workers who averaged £37 towards the end of the nineteenth century. In large, well-run, households the whole of the payment was disposable income - pocket money - as everything else, accommodation, food, was provided. Thus it proved possible for many servants to spend very little of what they received and some accrued substantial savings by the time they married. At least one historian has argued that they had a distinct wage advantage over other female workers because their living expenses were met. Not every domestic servant, of course, enjoyed such wealth and privileges as a teenage girl employed as a 'slavey' might receive only one shilling a week for her hard work.

Some historians have suggested that, despite its low pay, domestic service provided opportunities for social mobility. Young women allegedly perceived domestic service as a stepping stone to gentility because they were in contact with people who were perceived to be their social superiors. Similarly, domestic service was thought to provide a greater opportunity to marry well as respectable working-class men often preferred to marry servants who were trained in female domestic skills and thus made better wives. Oral testimonies indicate that ex-domestic servants were very particular about table manners, place settings and other social graces when bringing up their own children. Other historians disagree with this optimistic interpretation. According to one historian, marriage records indicate that servants were not upwardly mobile as they married into a similar social group as their parents. Domestic servants may have had access to middle-class mores but it is argued that it was a myth that they shared a middle-class lifestyle because servants were expected to work long hours, often from 6am to 10pm, carry out dirty, arduous and physically demanding tasks and be at the beck and call of their employers. Hannah Cullwick wrote in her diary on Saturday, 26 December, 1863

1 I light'd the fires and black'd the grates - the kitchen grate was so
greasy I'd to wash it over first. I felt glad the Christmas was over so
far. I clean'd two pair o' boots. Swept and dust'd the room and the
hall and got the breakfast up. The Missus came down into the
5 kitchen and look'd around at what was left and paid me my
quarter's wages (£2 in all) ... I clean'd the kitchen and passage and
the stairs and wash'd up in the scullery. Got the supper over and to
bed at 10.

Utterly dependent on employers, domestic servants had little personal
freedom. Employers were at liberty to interfere in their social lives or
discourage them from having 'followers' or boyfriends. Equally, sexual
harassment was an occupational hazard for domestic servants who had
often to cope with the unwelcome advances of men who lived or worked
in the household. In addition, aged, sick or pregnant servants were
unceremoniously dismissed to fend for themselves as employers were
not legally obliged to care for them.

By the end of the nineteenth century, domestic service appeared to be
in decline as only 35 per cent of the female workforce were classified as
such in 1911. Some historians have suggested that the decline of
domestic service was linked to the increase in job opportunities for
working-class women. It is argued that better educational provision,
particularly after 1870, promoted higher aspirations which left the
domestic service population an aging one. Others have argued that
domestic service declined because of a similar decrease in the
agricultural population. With the depopulation of rural areas there was
no army of labour on which to draw. Finally the increased cost of living,
the prohibitive expense of domestic service, the introduction of new
labour-saving devices as well as a decrease in the size of the middle-class
family encouraged many to economise and cut down on the number of
women they employed.

Of course, there may not have been a decline in domestic service after
all. Census enumerators often misrecorded women's work by
categorising all women in a household as domestic servants. For
example, waged farm workers and shop assistants who helped in the
house, matchbox makers, chain and lace makers, and those who worked
in the garment trade were often classified as domestic servants.
Furthermore contemporaries did not distinguish between a member of
the family who did housework in return for board and lodging and a paid
servant so sisters, aunts and nieces were often entered incorrectly on
census returns. There was, therefore, a vast misrepresentation of
women's work by census enumerators who sometimes counted women
as domestic servants when they were obviously employed in other
trades. Budding researchers need to be aware of these vast
discrepancies. By the late nineteenth century, census enumerators were
far more rigorous in cataloguing occupations. Outdoor laundry workers,

farm workers and shop assistants who helped in the home were no longer categorised as servants. So the decline in domestic service might be nothing more than greater precision by census enumerators who took more care in distinguishing between women's work.

d) Agricultural Work

Agriculture was also said to have declined as a result of technological innovation. Until mechanisation, farming had always been women's as well as men's work. Women generally worked in the ancillary jobs. They ran the dairy, milked the cows, fed the chickens, picked fruit and vegetables and helped out at harvest time; they worked in agricultural gangs, cleared land, hoed turnips, weeded, sowed seeds, gleaned and worked in the barns pitching hay. Seasonal workers, the hop pickers of London and Shropshire and the fruit pickers of Evesham, also contributed to the agricultural economy. It used to be assumed that mechanisation led to a decline in women's participation in agriculture but this interpretation has been revised because of new work on the census returns. Census enumerators, it is argued, grossly underestimated women's work in rural communities. This was because much of women's agricultural work went unrecorded because it was part time or seasonal. For example, census returns, which were generally recorded in the spring, did not record agricultural workers who took part in the August harvest.

In general terms, women also remained active in the dairy and other ancillary jobs until a later date than used to be supposed. For example, cheese making remained a traditional female job in the home until it was manufactured in factories in the 1870s. Furthermore, the notorious East Anglian gang system survived long into the late nineteenth century. Bands of agricultural workers, men, women and children, under the supervision of a 'gang master' were employed as casual labourers by farmers. These gangs roamed the countryside seeking work, slept in barns, sheds or in the fields and were paid daily 'piece rates'. As casual labour they were easily dismissed when the work had finished so that much of their work was unrecorded. Consequently, it is difficult to chart the numbers of female farm workers because of the inaccuracy of census returns. However, we do know that for agricultural workers such as these, the benefits of industrialisation were non-existent because their work continued to be characterised by long hours, poor pay and abominable working conditions.

e) Textile Workers

The cotton industry provides the historian with an excellent example of shifts in the sexual division of labour as a result of industrialisation.

Textile workers experienced dramatic changes because the sexual division of labour altered twice in a short space of historical time. As industrialisation proceeded, so spinning, traditionally a female job, became men's work and weaving, traditionally a male job, became women's work.

There had always been a sexual division of labour in the cotton industry. Both women and men worked in the textile trade but rarely did so on equal terms. In the pre-industrial economy, when textile workers worked at home, men worked as weavers whereas women did the spinning and children of the family cleaned and combed the materials. Although all the family contributed to the income of the home, it was the father, as the head of household, who organised and disciplined the family workforce and negotiated terms with the merchant clothier.

The development of new technology dramatically changed this domestic system. The invention of a much bigger spinning machine, the water frame, changed cotton production from a domestic system of industry to a factory-based one. Women and children left their homes to work as spinners, piecers and scavengers in Richard Arkwright's first factory at Cromford. Arkwright's factory employed approximately 300 women and children who were the wives and children of local lead miners, whose industry was in decline. When Arkwright built a second factory in 1776 workers were recruited from other areas and by 1780, there were approximately 5,000 women and children employed in the spinning mills.

When women and children first entered the mills they were employed at similar work to that which they had done at home, but this was not to last. In 1779 Crompton invented the 'mule' which produced a better thread than the spinning jenny. Until recently historians have concentrated on the impact of this technology on the development of the industry itself or on child labour. The category of gender has enabled historians to examine the mule in a different way. The invention of this machinery meant a crucial change in the sexual division of labour. Quite simply, men took over women's job as spinners. Explanations for this change in the sexual division of labour vary. Was it male physical strength? Were men more skilled? Did men make better overseers? Were men jealous of women's factory work? All of these questions have been posed by historians seeking to understand the changes in the sexual division of labour.

One historian, writing in the 1930s, maintained that strength and skill determined the sex of the worker. Crompton's 'mules' were heavy machines which required strongly built people to work them. Women, weaker, smaller and more delicate than men were unable to match male physical strength, so men took over. This early thesis was supported by research in the 1980s which suggested that skilled women spinners lost their well-paid position on the spinning jennies before the invention of the 'mule'. This was because employers, in an effort to raise productivity, increased the number of spindles on jennies which meant that greater physical strength was needed. This marked the end of female spinning as men began to take over women's jobs. Crompton's mule, it was argued, merely consolidated the trend towards male spinners. In addition, the 'mule' was a complicated piece of machinery which required sensitive handling. Highly skilled workers were needed to operate such a sophisticated invention. Women, through lack of training, did not possess the necessary skills so men replaced them.

This explanation was challenged by other historians. Not all women, it was argued, were physically weak. Many women had the strength to work heavy machinery: women miners worked underground shifting coal until 1842, domestic servants hauled coal buckets up and down stairs while chain makers forged heavy pieces of iron. In addition, men were seen to develop the strength they had partly because of the work they did. Working-class women were encouraged to develop manual dexterity whereas men were encouraged to be strong. Innate physical strength was therefore an inadequate explanation for the changes in the sexual division of labour. Similarly, the definition of mule spinning as a skilled job was challenged. The concept of skill, like the notion of strength, was seen by historians as a social construct which had more to do with definitions of what was male and what was female than of natural aptitude. Women's work, was usually characterised as unskilled whereas men's work was defined as skilled. For example, women who worked the spinning jenny were deemed unskilled whereas mule spinners, who were male, were defined as skilled. Skill definitions were therefore saturated with gender bias, for the work of women was deemed to be inferior simply because women did it.

Other historians suggested different reasons for the change in the sexual division of labour in the cotton industry. It was claimed that men replaced women spinners because of alterations in working patterns. Early factory spinners worked alone but as machines became increasingly complicated, assistants were necessary. One person alone could not work Crompton's sophisticated machine so mule spinners employed two or three assistants, called piecers, over whom they had direct authority, paying them out of their own wages. At the precise moment at which the spinners took on this supervisory role, men took over. Men were seen to be better supervisors than women because they held natural authority. And because spinning assistants were often members of the family, men's established social position in the home enabled them to take a leadership role in the mill.

Finally, some historians have argued that the change in the sexual division of labour occurred because men had more right to work than women. The invention of the mule in 1776 coincided with a period of peace in England: it was after the end of the American and before the beginning of the French wars. Men, enlisted or press-ganged into the forces, returned to England looking for work. In this heightened competition for jobs, the invention of the mule opened up job opportunities for men who soon sought to exclude women from mule spinning.

With the invention of Cartwright's loom, weaving too transferred from the home to the factory. Weaving had traditionally been men's work in the pre-industrial economy but women became the first power-loom weavers when weaving was mechanised. Historians recognised that, like the changes in the spinning industry, this was a consequence of several factors. Firstly, the position of the weavers was already in decline when mechanisation occurred as from about the 1790s unskilled immigrants and women spinners, some of whom had been displaced by the 'mule', became weavers. When weaving became mechanised these newly qualified women went to work in the factories where they were joined by the wives and daughters of distressed hand-loom weavers. Secondly, considerations of economy encouraged factory owners to employ women as factory workers: power-loom weavers were considered unskilled so were paid lower wages. As women accepted lower wages they were welcome additions to the workforce. Thirdly, factory owners perceived women as malleable and servile, necessary prerequisites for work which was bound by rules and regulations. Finally, the reluctance of male hand-loom weavers to break their tradition of working independently at home proved to be a lethal blow to male labour. As the Select Committee reported in 1834 ' ...no man would like to work in a power-loom, they do not like it, there is such a clattering and noise it would almost make some men mad; and next, he would have to submit to a discipline that a hand-loom weaver can never submit to.' Consequently, men resisted factory employment until poverty broke down all defences.

With so few employment opportunities in northern towns like Burnley, Nelson and Blackburn men returned to the weaving trade in the 1840s but they still earned more than women. What we can say with some certainty is that remuneration in the cotton industry was gender specific. In theory, because weavers were paid according to how much cloth they wove (called piece rates because workers were paid for the piece of cloth they had produced) women workers could earn as much as a male weaver, but in practice they still did not earn as much as men. Men tended to work more looms than women, wove broad and heavy cloth which earned higher piece rates, tuned and adjusted their own looms, broke factory regulations by cleaning their looms in their breaks, and worked overtime. And, most importantly, men, not women, were promoted to overseers or managers.

As industrialisation proceeded so the differentiation between men's and women's jobs increased. In the domestic economy all the members of a family worked and were expected to contribute to the total income. With wages paid to individual workers, and higher ones paid to men, the concept of the 'family wage' paid to the male breadwinner developed.

The 'family wage' was thought to help working-class families because it was to be sufficient for husbands to keep their wives and family at home, but it had the effect of marginalising women's economic status still further. For women, it was a vicious circle of economic dependency. Women's paid work was considered less important than men's because it was low waged; as it paid less well than men's, women could not afford to support themselves and were forced into marriage through economic necessity; once married, they produced children and often stopped work. As women could never be breadwinners they usually stopped work to look after their family, thus increasing their reliance on a male income. Consequently, men assumed responsibility for the health, wealth and welfare of the family and soon demanded the protection of women workers and their exclusion from trade unions.

f) Coalmining Women: the Case of Protective Legislation

The picture of a almost-naked women crawling on all fours dragging a truck of coal in the dark, dusty and sweaty atmosphere of a mine was a reproach to the morality of Victorian England (see below). In 1842 the Children's Employment Commission underlined these dreadful working conditions. The revelations in this report, with its striking illustrations of women and children working in sub-human conditions, shocked contemporary society. Subsequently the Mines and Collieries Act banned women and children from working underground. With a genteel sigh of relief, Victorians patted themselves on their humanitarian backs for their zealousness in protecting women from degradation, or so many text books would have us believe. To enter the debate about protective legislation, however, is to enter - as one historian has remarked - a 'conceptual mine-field'. According to some, humanitarianism acted as a stimulus to protective legislation which was seen to benefit

Women in the mines

women. On the other hand, historians on the left of the political spectrum suggest that protective legislation was also a Tory and/or capitalist conspiracy passed either to protect the new-style Conservative party or the family from disintegration. Finally, some radical feminist historians argue that it was a none too subtle patriarchal plot whereby the male state, the male government and the male worker colluded to protect their masculine interests against the overwhelming surge of women into paid work.

So who benefited? Perhaps not women. Only 200 of 4,200 Scottish ex-colliery women had found work by 1845. With no employment many faced serious distress. Some relied on the notorious Poor Law, or when that was unavailable, charity. Others were supported by their families, went into service or hawked goods around farms. Although women in various regions of the country responded differently to unemployment their situation was disturbingly similar: they were poverty stricken. Some women tried to get back into the pits disguised as men or evaded the act in other ways. This placed coalmining women in an increasingly vulnerable position because they were working illegally. Mine owners were fined for breaking the 1842 law but fines were low and mine owners, anticipating a fine, deducted money from women's wages to cover the future cost of prosecution. State regulation, designed to protect women, instead forced them into unregulated, overcrowded and underpaid work.

Protective legislation had far more severe long-term effects on the position of women economically and socially. The Mines and Collieries Act, by viewing women in a similar way as children, in effect classified women as minors. Being designated as minor, women were defined as dependent persons who were incapable of looking after themselves rather than as mature adults.

So if women were not protected by the legislation, who were? Did the Tories and the capitalists benefit? Lord Ashley (who was later called Lord Shaftesbury) and Richard Oastler, who were both instrumental in passing the Mines and Collieries Act, were Tories committed to a degree of social reform. Some historians argue that these new-style Tories, under Peel, benefited by their association with reform. Peel recognised that the Reform Act of 1832 had created a distinctly new electorate which needed to be wooed and cajoled into voting Conservative. He was aware that the protection of women and children was a popular election issue, so in his Tamworth Manifesto of 1834 he promised voters some measure of social reform and thus attracted the support of the new middle-class electorate. Peel's commitment to protective legislation, some historians have alleged, halted the erstwhile disintegration of the Tory party, made many confident in the 1841-46 ministry of Peel and protected the government against the onslaught of new democratic forces.

Furthermore, it was argued, the economic system of capitalism needed a disciplined, regularised workforce in order to maximise profit.

Miners were notoriously independent, took off 'St Monday' and did not work regular hours. Revolution was also feared. The 1840s marked a period of revolutions in Europe, violent Chartist upheavals, strike action and other working-class disturbances such as the Plug and Rebecca riots. It was believed, by influential figures such as Lord Shaftesbury, that this insubordination occurred as a result of the disintegration of the family. Some women historians have agreed with nineteenth-century contemporary opinion and have maintained that the family was an institution which maintained and perpetuated the capitalist system. By reproducing labour power, by constituting the major unit of consumption, by socialising the young and by providing an arena of emotional support, the family has been viewed as an essential component in the success of capitalism. Coalmining women threatened the family and with it the social fabric of society by asserting their independence, drinking in pubs, swearing, working naked and neglecting their domestic duties. It was argued that this unwillingness to espouse traditional values made coal mining women unsuitable wives and mothers.

Protective legislation offered a solution to these problems. Men, it was hoped, would be less likely to take days off, engage in strike action, riot or demonstrate if they were responsible for the welfare of their families. It was in the employers' collective interest to support protective legislation. With women returned to domesticity the family could provide a bulwark against riot and revolution, and persuade reluctant men to keep working. Indeed, there was strong evidence from the pits where women had been excluded that it did have a steadying impact on the male miners.

Many feminists became dissatisfied with a Marxist analysis and replaced this with the idea of patriarchy. It was argued that working men feared women's infiltration into industry because it took away their jobs, lowered their wages, diminished male authority, and marked a deterioration in home life. Protective legislation gave men back their rightful place in the scheme of work, for it contributed to the idea that women should work only under exceptional circumstances. This in turn made it impossible for a working woman to survive materially without a male breadwinner. Low female wages forced women into marriage, a relationship within which their husbands could expect a whole range of unpaid services. Thus the male worker, ever fearful of the feminine threat, colluded with the capitalists, supported protective legislation and campaigned for the family wage. Women on the other hand were trapped.

Some historians would argue that these different ideas imposed a theoretical orthodoxy on a rather chaotic practice. First of all, some women were 'protected' by legislation and were no doubt relieved to stop working in damp, dark, dank mines even though they suffered from low pay and unemployment as a result. Secondly, protective legislation was not a clear-cut party question. Not all Tories supported legislation for it eroded their dearly held principles of *laissez faire*. Similarly not all mine owners favoured women working underground: those who owned larger, sophisticated, mines tended to support government intervention, whilst those who owned technologically backward mines tended to oppose legislation. Large mines, which made a healthy profit, were well able to afford the higher wages of skilled male workers whereas smaller mines depended on cheaper female and child labour to maintain their profit margins. Thirdly, attitudes towards women coalminers varied across the country: there was no coherent working-class response to protective legislation. Some coalminers wished to prohibit women working underground whereas others preferred to have their wives and daughters working alongside them. Consequently, one is led to believe that the Mines and Collieries Act was the result of diverse pressures from social reformers, working men, employers and politicians rather than simply a patriarchal plot or capitalist conspiracy.

Until 1853 protective legislation usually applied to the mines and the textile factories. Sweatshop workers who regularly worked a 70-hour week and many others remained unprotected. Although Acts in 1853, 1860, 1864, 1867, 1878, 1891, and 1895 extended the protection of the textile trade to other industries, they did not cover every occupation. Not until 1909 did the Trades Board Acts establish wage boards for women chain makers, lace makers, bespoke tailoring and paper box making. Domestic service remained unregulated.

2 Women and Trade Unions

Women joined unions for the same reasons as men: to campaign for better pay, shorter hours and improved working conditions. Nevertheless, the women's story was different from men's and their struggle was much harder. Consequently, women's unionisation was weak, sporadic and, all too often, ineffective.

This section will examine the difficulties women faced in joining a union before exploring the ways in which women managed to develop their own organisations.

a) The Difficulties of Joining a Union

Women were not taken seriously as union members because they were rarely seen as a permanent part of the wage economy. Unlike men, women did not begin work at the age of 10 and finish when they were too old to continue, but often ceased work when they married. Women were therefore perceived as wives and mothers more than workers and were called 'mean-time' workers because work was considered a temporary stop gap between childhood and motherhood.

In addition, the dual burden of home and work made it difficult for women to fit in a union meeting between cleaning, cooking and baking and certainly did not have the spare time available to listen to the long speeches made at such meetings. Moreover, union meetings were held outside working hours, often in pubs or clubs which were not considered respectable places for a woman to be. With no alternative venue of their own, women were effectively excluded from participating in union politics.

Women also earned less than men so found it difficult to pay union fees. The relegation of women to low-paid work certainly prohibited them from affording the high dues and subscription rates to the unions which dominated the first three-quarters of the nineteenth century. Historians have also argued that it was difficult to collect subscriptions from women as large numbers worked in small workshops which meant that union stewards were forced to walk long distances to collect weekly payments. Domestic servants were notoriously difficult to unionise, not only because they worked in individual houses but because they were so deferential to their employers.

Finally, the hostility of many male trade unionists prohibited women organising. Women were often seen as rivals in the workplace and as an economic threat rather than partners in a struggle against an exploitative employer. The Northern Star, a leading Chartist newspaper in the 1840s pleaded that women stay at home so that there would be less pressure on the labour market. Indeed, Henry Broadhurst, President of the TUC, said in 1877 that 'it was their duty as men and husbands to use their utmost efforts to bring about a condition of things, where their wives would be in their proper sphere at home, instead of being dragged into competition for livelihood against the great and strong men of the world'. Consequently, many male trade unionists sought to stop women working by rigidly controlling entry to skilled work. They also supported the family wage and protective legislation in order to protect their position in the labour market. Coalmining women were successfully banned from working underground but attempts were also made to exclude women from nail making, chain making and working on the pit brow. Because women were denied entry to work they were, of course, ineligible to join a union. Furthermore, men excluded women who did work from their trade unions. In 1829 at a conference of textile workers in the Isle of Man women were excluded from joining a newly formed union. John Doherty, the leader, stated that 'no person or persons be learned or allowed to spin except the son, brother, or orphan nephew of spinners'. Indeed, as late as 1914 when several unions united to form the National Union of Railwaymen, women were not allowed to join - even though they had been members of one of the previous unions. Only 40 per cent of unions had accepted women by 1921: the Amalgamated Society of Engineers did not allow women members until 1943. As there were very few female unions at the time it was exceedingly difficult for women to unionise but they did achieve some success in the textile trades.

However, it must be remembered that men as well as women found it difficult to form unions throughout most of the nineteenth century. Both employers and governments considered unions a threat and sought to hamper their growth through restrictive legislation. In 1799 the Combination Acts made all unions illegal and even when these Acts were repealed in 1824 it remained difficult to join a union. Thus the story of women's trade unions between 1800 and 1870 has to be viewed within the context of government repression and legislation. In the 1870s, when trade unions were legalised, women's unions enjoyed greater success.

b) The Development of Women's Unions

The majority (75 per cent) of women trade unionists were textile workers, for fairly obvious reasons. Firstly, large numbers of women were employed in the textile trade for it was the single largest employer outside of domestic service. Secondly, textile workers were employed in factories which were easier to organise than the small isolated workshops in which women traditionally worked. Thirdly, textile workers belonged to close-knit communities with unusual traditions of solidarity with husbands, wives, sons and daughters often belonging to the same union branch. Most importantly of all, female textile workers were relatively well paid so could afford the subscription rates.

Even so, there were considerable regional variations in women's experiences. Some local textile unions welcomed women members. In a few places women paid the same subscription rates and enjoyed the same benefits as men. In Oldham and Derby, areas with a history of sexually mixed unions, women were involved in riotous confrontations with employers and police, and, like the men, fought, stoned and intimidated strike breakers. As members of the Manchester Spinners and the Manchester Small Weavers Societies they drew strike pay, in 1818, on the same basis as male workers. In 1837 the Bolton Association negotiated favourable piece rates which meant that equal pay became a theoretical reality but as women tended to work on fewer looms so equal pay rarely occurred in practice.

Textile workers were not the only ones who attempted to unionise. When Robert Owen tried to federate all unions into his impressively titled Grand National Consolidated Trade Union (GNCTU) in 1834 it attracted a large number of women. Separate lodges of The Ancient Virgins, the Lodge of Female Tailors, the Female Gardeners, the Ancient Shepherdesses were formed under its collectivist umbrella. After the collapse of the GNCTU many trade unionists turned to Chartism to solve their political problems and unionism, as a whole, became quiescent until the 1870s.

Historians agree that the decades after the 1870s formed a significant watershed for the growth of trade unions in general and for those of the unskilled and low paid in particular. In some ways, women's unions paralleled the development of male unionism which flourished at this time, but there were many differences. Both men and women were helped by a loosening of the regulations surrounding trade unions but women gained additional support from influential middle-class sympathisers who devoted their lives to improving the lives of working-class women.

Emma Paterson, Lady Dilke, Gertrude Tuckwell and Annie Besant were amongst many middle-class female reformers who strove to improve conditions for the working class. For example, Emma Paterson formed the Women's Protective and Provident League (WPPL), which later became the Women's Trade Union League, to help women form their own unions. The WPPL supported and organised all-women unions because it believed mixed unions denied women important opportunities. In mixed unions, there were few, if any, women at the top whereas single-sex unions enabled women to gain confidence and encouraged them to become leaders.

The WPPL was one of the first organisations to promote the cause of working-class women but it has a curious history. It began as a feminist organisation but as the years passed it placed a higher priority on socialist ideals. In its early years, under the Presidency of Emma Patterson, the WPPL was considered to be a relatively respectable institution because it believed in conciliation rather than confrontation. Its name - the Women's Protective and Provident League - reflected these placatory politics: it avoided the word 'union' in case it upset its wealthy supporters. Not surprisingly it disapproved of strike action. It has been suggested that the WPPL was a heady mixture of feminism, philanthropy and respectable trade unionism. Its feminist perspective encouraged it to oppose protective legislation because it implied that women lacked the capacity to look after themselves. Indeed, Emma Patterson believed that a male Parliament had little right to pass laws which affected disenfranchised women. The WPPL's philanthropic background was reflected in the ways in which it gave financial assistance to newly formed unions, helped in advertising, convened meetings and gave advice about organisation and administration. Finally, a respectable trade union image was nourished by the high priority given by the WPPL to welfare benefits. Indeed, by providing a wide range of facilities for its members such as a bank, a reading room, a library, a swimming club as well as an employment register, the WPPL was criticised for being more of a friendly society than a union.

Under the leadership of Lady Emilia Dilke, who became President after Emma Patterson's death, the WPPL not only changed its name to the Women's Trade Union League (WTUL) but changed its politics and policies. As it entered its socialist phase, the WTUL encouraged strike action, abandoned its antagonism towards protective legislation and became the female equivalent of the Trades Union Congress. This marked change in attitude towards strike action augured well for the success of the well-known Match Girls' strike in 1888, for the WTUL put its organisation at the disposal of the match 'girls', collected £400 in strike funds and encouraged them to form a union. In turn, this strike inspired other women to establish unions. During the 1890s the WTUL helped spread unionism to shop assistants, clerks and other non-unionised labour and approximately 80-90 different unions were founded under the auspices of the WTUL. However, during this socialist phase, mothers were discouraged from working outside the home, family values were upheld and support for protective legislation grew. This change in direction reflected the WTUL's new roots in the trade union movement rather than in middle-class philanthropy and made it more attractive to male trade unionists who began to support women's membership. Consequently, in 1889, the WTUL encouraged women to join existing unions rather than set up separate organisations. Unions which accepted female members affiliated to the WTUL which in turn provided speakers and organisers to help recruitment. By the 1890s 60 unions had affiliated to the WTUL and the TUC supported equal pay which made it seem as if the animosity between men and women workers was ending.

An alternative organisation, the Women's Trade Union Association (WTUA), was founded because of dissatisfaction with the WTUL and marked a shift from middle-class philanthropic support to male working-class support. The WTUA was founded in 1889 by Clementina Black as a radical substitute to the WTUL and attracted the support of male radicals rather than middle-class philanthropists. Influential left-wing trade unionists such as John Burns, Ben Tillett and Tom Mann supported the WTUL because it organised amongst the sweated workers of the East End. Rope makers, confectioners, box makers, shirt makers, umbrella makers and brush makers were all recruited to this new association. In 1889, supported by Burns and dockyard workers, the WTUA won an important victory at the Allen Chocolate Makers. However, the WTUA was less effective outside London and by the mid 1890s it was less dynamic. Eventually in 1897 it merged with the Women's Industrial Council, a research and educational organisation which saw itself as a watchdog body which campaigned for a minimum wage, encouraged Wage Boards and supported government intervention.

Despite the efforts of the WPPL and the WTUA, the vast majority of women workers had no union to join. To remedy this, Mary MacArthur, a leading figure within the WPPL/WTUL, set up the National Federation of Women Workers (NFWW) in 1906. This federation recruited women workers from previously unorganised trades and amalgamated the many small unions founded by the WPPL. Although there was liaison between the NFWW and the WTUL, common membership, and shared leaders, the two groups offered contrasting services and worked in diverse ways. The NFWW was considerably more radical than most of the older unions. Modelling itself on general labour unions it offered low subscription rates and financial backing for strikes. The NFWW emerged at a time of great industrial, social and political unrest: the 'troubles' in Ireland, an intransigent House of Lords, the suffrage movement and increased strike action by militant trade unionists all caused problems for the Liberal government. It has even been suggested that much of the industrial disturbance that characterised this period, particularly in the Black Country and London, was created by women. To some extent this was engendered by the NFWW which launched a two-pronged attack on the government and employers.

The leader of the NFWW, Mary MacArthur, helped to found an Anti-Sweating League which put pressure on the Liberal government to pass a Trades Boards Act of 1909. This Act established four Boards of employers and employees who were empowered to fix minimum wages for chain making, lace making, paper box making and bespoke tailoring. From August 1910, approximately 2,000 women chain makers were therefore legally entitled to the new rates of two and a half old pence an hour. Employers tried to subvert the law by persuading chain makers to sign agreements stating that they were willing to forgo their rights. Those refusing to sign were locked out. By September almost 800 women were locked out and the chain makers' strike was the inevitable consequence.

The successful end to this strike can be directly attributed to Julia Varley, a Birmingham NFWW organiser who adopted the methods of the suffrage movement and produced highly visual propaganda to publicise the plight of the chain makers. This gained them support from both the local and national press and inspired the three other trades to persuade employers to increase their pay to legal standards. Between 1906 and 1920 the NFWW organised large numbers of strikes to gain a minimum wage for other groups of sweated workers. During the summer months of 1911 a variety of women workers - jam and pickle makers, rag pickers, bottle washers and tin box makers - went on strike, all of which contributed to the great industrial unrest which was symptomatic of the period before the Great War.

Despite widespread trade union action, women's employment prospects at the outbreak of war remained grim as they were still expected to be wives and mothers rather than workers. The economic upshot of this was that women's work remained characterised by low pay, long hours and poor conditions with women locked into a circle of deprivation. Even in the midst of war, when unions such as the Kidderminster Power Loom, Carpet Weaving and Textile Workers

Association eventually allowed women to join, one historian has noted that women were still not given equal rights - twenty-five women's votes were counted for one man's.

3 Towards Emancipation: Middle-class Women and Work

There were at least two labour markets for women in Victorian Britain. One of them catered for working-class women and a second existed for the middle class. Occupations deemed suitable for working-class women were thought unsuitable for the middle class so the history of middle-class women's work contrasts sharply with that of the working class. At the same time as working-class women's job opportunities were restricted, middle-class women demanded greater participation in the workforce. In the early part of the century middle-class women were expected to withdraw from work and remain in the home, but by the latter part of the century they were campaigning to be accepted in traditionally male jobs. By 1900 middle-class women were enjoying the right to be employed in previously male-dominated professions. This section will explore some of these changes.

a) Middle-class Women's Exclusion from Work

Middle-class women were less likely to take an active part in the economy in 1830 than they had in 1750 because of changes in the nature of businesses such as retailing. In the late eighteenth century, for example, owners usually lived above their shop. Wives were responsible for housekeeping and raising the children but they also worked in the shop, supervised the apprentices and ran the business in their husband's absence or after their husband's death. This was not to be the case for their sons and their wives, a change which occurred for a number of reasons.

First of all, the separation of home from work decreased women's opportunity to participate in the workforce. Shop owners ceased to live above the shop, moving out to new middle-class suburbs. As a consequence, two separate spheres emerged. Home was increasingly regarded as the woman's place, whereas work was more and more thought to be the man's place. With the growth of this domestic ideology (the idea that men go out to work whereas women stay at home) it was thought unseemly for middle-class women to work outside the home.

Another reason for women's diminishing involvement in the world of work was a change in the nature and the size of the business enterprise. Before the advent of limited liability in 1856 many businesses were family owned and financed. Wives, mothers and sisters all helped finance the family business. George Courtauld, a silk manufacturer, borrowed large sums from his sister and lived off his wife's dowry in order to reinvest the factory profits. The growth of the private company, the development of banking and formal financial procedures changed the way in which businesses like Courtaulds were managed. The decline of independent workshops and the takeover of many family firms by larger companies resulted in women's removal from the workplace and spelt doom for unmarried female entrepreneurs because they were excluded from the newer financial world.

Older family firms catered for a local clientele, whereas the new business enterprises were drawn into a regional or even a national market. This expansion of trade created a need for greater physical mobility which in turn excluded women because it was considered inappropriate for middle-class ladies to travel unchaperoned. Larger businesses employed a bigger, masculine and semi-skilled workforce. In the past women had played an important role in caring for apprentices, particularly in the cotton trade, but the gradual demise of child labour diminished their involvement. Supervising an ever increasing semi-skilled male adult workforce was considered unsuitable for women, so they gradually withdrew to the home.

The nature of jobs also changed. Early nineteenth-century health care was often in the hands of women who gathered and grew the herbs which were the basis of most remedies. For instance, Mrs Boot, the mother of the founder of Boots the chemist, brewed herbal medicines for sale in the back of her house in Nottingham. With the professionalisation of medicine women's role in health and welfare declined. New technological and scientific improvements also discriminated against women. The introduction of steam powered machinery in agriculture allegedly excluded women because they did not have the scientific or technical knowledge essential to manage its implementation.

Other jobs disappeared. Essex and Suffolk, for instance, shifted from mixed to arable farming which resulted in a loss of female jobs. Previously, women supervised the dairy, using the labour of their daughters, nieces and live-in dairy maids to help. Arable farming, with its emphasis on corn and cattle, superseded mixed farming and made women's expertise redundant. Inn keeping, an important occupation for widows, also declined. Growing social disapproval of alcohol consumption combined with railway development (inns were used as coaching stations) meant that women were less likely to be found in this occupation. Nevertheless, the decline in women's employment was uneven for there were certainly distinct regional differences. For instance, women remained working in agriculture in very rural areas, particularly on smaller farms, for much longer than previously supposed.

b) Opportunities for Middle-class Women

However, a considerable number of middle-class women were forced to seek paid work. Many of these occupations were based on the domestic ideology, posed little threat to the masculine world of work and merely reinforced women's caring and nurturing role.

(i) The Teaching Profession

Large numbers of single women, considered a financial burden on their families, were encouraged to seek work as governesses. In 1851 there were approximately 25,000 of them in England alone. It was a job, like domestic service, that accorded perfectly with that of wife and mother and posed no threat to men. It was also characterised by poor pay and low esteem as in the late 1840s the average wage was between £20 to £45 per annum which compared unfavourably with housekeepers who earned between £40-£50. In Charlotte Bronte's novel *Jane Eyre* it is possible to glimpse what life was like for many governesses, epitomised by this particularly sad figure of historical fiction.

Although governesses were technically servants they occupied an ambiguous position in the family home as the following account written in 1865 suggests:

> ... the real discomfort of a governess's position in a private family arises from the fact that it is undefined. She is not a relation, not a guest, not a mistress, not a servant - but something made up of all. No one knows exactly how to treat her.

Governesses tended to come from the more privileged sector of society rather than the working class. Consequently they pierced the conscience of do-gooding families and elicited far more concern from the press and philanthropists than domestic servants. Victorians wrote endlessly about the poor treatment meted out to governesses and set up various charities to support them. The Governesses' Benevolent Institution provided much-needed financial assistance in sickness, unemployment and retirement. Emigration societies were founded to encourage governesses to work abroad. For those, and there were many, unable to gain such assistance life was far grimmer. Some ended their days in the workhouse or asylums: apparently there were more governesses than any other female occupation in lunatic asylums.

Teachers held a higher status than governesses but women entered the teaching profession for similar reasons. Teaching was considered a respectable job because the education of children was perceived to be an extension of women's natural childrearing role. At the beginning of the nineteenth century teaching needed few resources and little training to enter. Middle-class married women often owned and ran schools

alongside their husbands, although it was usually men who officially owned them. Single women, left an annuity or small inheritance, set up schools in their local community, usually taking in lower-middle-class girls to be educated as wives and mothers. The expansion of working-class education throughout the nineteenth century created new opportunities for middle-class women. School mistresses on the fringes of the lower-middle-class found the National or British and Foreign schools attractive. Similarly, the Education Act of 1870, which gave local areas the opportunity to build Board Schools, gave an important impetus to the career of teaching. Initially, posts in the newly built Board Schools were filled by working-class applicants but gradually teaching attracted the middle class. From the 1890s universities trained teachers from a middle-class background which led to a corresponding decline in the number of pupil-teachers who had been drawn from the ranks of the working class.

Despite a growth in teaching opportunities, women's role was circumscribed by the gender ideology of the day. Pay remained gender specific: Witham National School was typical of most schools when it offered £55 for a master and £35 for a mistress in 1840. Equal pay for equal work was not a possibility in the nineteenth-century teaching profession. Opportunities for promotion were equally scarce. Some women gained jobs as heads of infant schools or of girls' elementary schools but most heads were men. To add to this inequality, women were invariably dismissed from their posts when they married, even though this was not mandatory until the 1920s when a formal marriage bar applied to women teachers. In spite of this, a small number of talented individuals joined the local inspectorate and an exceptional few joined the staff of the newly created teacher training colleges. Not surprisingly many of the teacher training heads became suffragists. Nonetheless, women were notably absent from the universities and Her Majesty's Inspectorate both of which tended to recruit men from the public schools and Oxbridge.

(ii) Other White-collar Workers

The expansion of the employment of middle-class women in the white-collar, or what was often termed the 'white-blouse', industry was dramatic. Women replaced men in a variety of jobs but, as with cotton weavers, these occupations declined in status and pay when women took over. In the early part of the century few women were employed as shop assistants, clerical workers or civil servants. By 1911, this had changed with 366,268 employed as shop assistants and 39,773 as civil servants. This shift took place for two main reasons. Firstly, the expansion of the retail trade, the business sector and the civil service created additional jobs and, secondly, the nature of these jobs changed. The new white collar workers tended to be viewed as less skilled, were consequently lower paid and were thus viewed as appropriate jobs for women.

Women had been associated with shopkeeping for years but as co-owners rather than assistants. A number of famous shops, not just Boots, were begun by women. The firm of H. Samuel was named after Harriet who began the business in 1863 and the Lansdowne laundry in Birmingham grew out of the laundry work of a woman who took in washing of the wealthy. At the beginning of the nineteenth century, there were few paid shop assistants, male or female, as most retail shops were privately owned and staffed by family members. By the latter part of the century, shops had increased in both number and size with newly built department stores employing hundreds of shop assistants. With the rapid growth of retail trade in the latter part of the nineteenth century, more and more middle-class women (and indeed upper-working-class women) found employment in high-prestige department stores. Shop assistants in large department stores required limited training, were designated unskilled workers and were lower paid than men. Women congregated in drapery, millinery, women's fashion, and confectionery where work was light and where customers were mostly women.

Clerical work changed for similar reasons. In the early part of the nineteenth century most businesses, like shops, were family-run establishments. Clerks, drawn from the men of the middle classes, were apprenticed and employed by small businesses to deal with the administrative work. These young men had sufficient education to equip them to read, write and do simple accounts. Nonetheless, in the second half of the century, business and commerce expanded and changed. The growth of administrative structures in industry and commerce led to new job opportunities for women. Clerical work became mechanised, de-professionalised and some would argue, proletarianised as it became less skilled and less well paid. With the invention of the typewriter (female typists were initially called typewriters) which was considered to be suited to women's manual dexterity, the number of women clerks increased dramatically.

The development of the Civil Service created further job opportunities for women. At the beginning of the century the Civil Service dealt mainly with defence and law and order but by 1911 it had increased out of all recognition. A new collectivist State with its education, health and welfare systems required a larger body of staff to administer it. Posts which had previously been distributed by patronage were advertised and recruited through open competitive examinations. One of the State's biggest organisations, the Post Office, apparently employed 90 per cent of civil servants and the largest number of middle-class women. However, the majority of women civil servants worked in the lower grades as telephonists, telegraphists and typists rather than administrators. Only a very few entered the inspectorate, inspecting schools, factories and workshops, workhouses and even by 1914 women inspectors only numbered about 200.

In contrast to other white-collar workers, the working day of the civil servant was shorter, they enjoyed sick leave and annual holidays. Until 1946, however, women were dismissed on marriage, forfeited their pension rights and instead received a gratuity or a dowry, if they had worked for more than six years. In 1961 they obtained equal pay with men, fourteen years before it became law under the Sex Discrimination Act of 1975.

(iii) Philanthropy

Large numbers of upper- and middle-class women found employment in the unpaid work of philanthropy. A bevy of domestic servants freed middle-class women from their home responsibilities and gave them the opportunity to engage in good works. Instead of remaining in their own private sphere, cleaning their own homes, cooking their own meals and bringing up their own children, many middle-class women spent some of their time in helping others. Such women engaged in a wide variety of charitable work. They rescued and reformed prostitutes, visited gaols, orphanages and workhouses and worked in missionary societies and temperance movements. They even set up training homes for domestic servants. For many women, charitable work was a full-time, albeit unpaid, job as this extract from Elizabeth Cadbury's diary, written in May 1899 demonstrates:

> Morning, separate sitting on Position of Women. Miss Richardson lunch with me. Afternoon, Education question in joint sitting; much diversity; I spoke. Evening, Home Missions.

Victorian England also witnessed the revival of Anglican sisterhoods of nuns. In 1845 the first Anglican order called the Park Village Sisters was founded and was swiftly followed by a number of others. By 1900, 54 new orders had been created with a membership of between 2,000-3,000 women. Religious communities attracted women because they were an extension of charitable work - under the aegis of the Church a single woman could become a nurse, a social worker or even a foreign missionary.

On the one hand, charitable work reaffirmed women's subordinate position within Victorian England. It was often seen as an extension of the home. Looking after children, the sick, the old, the infirm and the socially deprived was woman's sphere. Because charity was unpaid work women still relied on the financial support of husbands or fathers. Consequently the social order remained undisputed. On the other hand, charity work cast doubt upon the status quo. It enabled middle-class women to gain experience in public speaking, commercial expertise in running charitable organisations, a measure of financial acumen, and administrative, marketing and social welfare skills. This challenged the middle-class version of the sexual division of labour because charity work demonstrated that women were competent managers. Historians have argued that the involvement of middle-class women in philanthropy made a significant impact on social policy in that they were the architects of modern welfare systems. For example, women visitors to workhouses allegedly facilitated changes in the Poor Law when they voiced concern about the dreadful conditions in these institutions. Furthermore charitable work emancipated middle-class women from their own personal domestic environment which, combined with the skills they acquired, could be used to challenge the social, economic and political order should they wish. For example, many women who were involved in the suffrage campaign cut their political teeth in charitable work. It also gave women the expertise and confidence to apply for paid jobs as social workers in the emerging welfare state of the early twentieth century.

c) Changes in Middle-class Women's Work

Charity, however, could not solve women's employment problems. Political activists tried to increase job prospects for women by founding the Association for the Promotion of the Employment of Women in the late 1850s. This organisation established an employment register, a printing establishment, classes in book-keeping, a law-copying office, and an office for tracing architectural plans. SPEW, as it became known, relied on charitable donations for its work but, unfortunately, received insufficient financial support so failed in its major aim. One historian has noted that SPEW was more a centre of propaganda than an employment exchange. Middle-class women achieved more in their campaigns to gain entry into the medical profession.

Before the 1850s the stereotypical image of the nurse was of someone who was illiterate, uneducated, gin-sodden, sexually promiscuous, incompetent, untrained and completely incapable. Nurses were said to begin their shift drunk and disorderly, they stole pillows, blankets and food from patients and behaved in inappropriate ways. One matron recalled that 'The nurses were drawn from the lowest denizens of the surrounding neighbourhood, such as preferred sick nursing to street walking, and perhaps they were able to combine the two trades'. More importantly they were working class. By 1900 this image of nursing had altered, a change instigated by the work of Florence Nightingale. After establishing a formidable reputation in the Crimea, Nightingale returned to England to found the first nurse training school at St Thomas's Hospital, London in 1860. It had a two-fold aim. First of all, Nightingale hoped to make nursing a respectable profession and, secondly, she wanted to train nurses in medical care. Nightingale therefore recruited women with high moral character, and trained them in respectable behaviour as well as in medical knowledge. Monthly reports were sent to her on each of her student nurses. She invited comments upon the personal neatness, quietness, sobriety, honesty and nursing accomplishments of each of her students to ensure that they met her exacting moral standards. Probationary nurses followed a rigid daily regime which taught them the rudiments of medical care. They worked from 6am to 10pm, helped in the wards, attended medical classes, took case notes and studied medical texts. Other nurse training schools were established which advocated similar behavioural and academic standards. Class divisions were maintained in these hospitals. 'Ladies' were not expected to perform the menial tasks such as cleaning spittoons, they had private rooms in the nursing home, ate separately, and often wore a distinctive uniform. Even though salaries remained low - Matrons earned £100, sisters £30 and nurses £20 in the 1890's - nursing attracted hundreds of applicants for the few places available in prestigious training hospitals. This perhaps tells us more about the lack of job opportunities than it does about women's nursing vocation. By 1881, there were 35,715 trained nurses.

A few women tried to become doctors. This was not an easy task because, unlike nursing, it threatened male jobs. The first woman doctor, Elizabeth Blackwell, who had gained her degree at an American university was swiftly struck of the British Medical Register because it was feared that other women might study at foreign universities in order to practise in Britain. It took the joint efforts of Elizabeth Garrett Anderson and Sophia Jex-Blake to get women admitted into Medical Schools in Britain. But even though women were allowed to enrol at medical college they were not always made welcome. Male students at Edinburgh rioted, cat-called and swore at prospective candidates. On one occasion a few students pushed a sheep in after the women. Fortunately, a sympathetic lecturer remarked 'Leave it, leave it, it is more intelligent than those who drove it in'. Despite the support of such men, it remained difficult for women to qualify as doctors as only a few hospitals would accept them as trainees.

Similar campaigns were organised for women lawyers, factory, health and sanitation inspectors, administrators, artists and journalists, although not so energetically as for medicine. Not until the outbreak of war in 1914 - when women began to be employed as bus drivers, engineers, coalsweepers, agricultural workers, electricians and such like - were women of both the working and middle class employed in traditionally male jobs.

Making notes on '*Women and Work*'

This chapter has been divided into three sections which should provide an overall structure for your notes. Your notes on women's work should enable you to assess the significant changes as well as the continuities in women's work during industrialisation. You need to think about the changes and the continuities in women's work, the extent to which a sexual division of labour was detrimental to women and whether or not protective legislation was beneficial.

The following headings may help you with notetaking:

Working class women's work

1. Effect of industrialisation
   a) You need to understand the views of the optimists and the pessimists with regard to women's work.
   b) Make sure that you understand that women's work remained unaffected by industrialisation in many areas such as home-working.

2. Domestic service

Most working women were employed as domestic servants. Although there were various jobs undertaken by domestic servants, they shared much in common. Domestic service was low paid and reinforced women's traditional role as home-maker. Historians disagree on whether domestic service provided opportunities for social mobility.

3. Agricultural work

To what extent did agricultural work decline as a result of industrialisation?

4. Cotton workers

One of the crucial changes in the textile trade was the change in the sexual division of labour. This section enables you to explore the reasons for this change. Why did the sexual division of labour change in the spinning trade? Was it strength? Was it skill? Was it because the machines were complicated? Was it because men needed work? Do the same reasons apply for the changes in the weaving trade?

5. Protective legislation

Historians differ about whether or not protective legislation was a good thing. Some insist that women benefited from protective legislation. Others disagree. The disagreements, to some extent, reflect political differences. Socialist historians have tended to favour interpretations which indicate that capitalism benefited from protective legislation whereas radical feminist historians have preferred to view men as the beneficiaries.

Trade Unions

This section considers the reasons why it was difficult for women to unionise and examines the reasons for the limited success of women's unions.

Middle-class women and work

a) This section examines the role of middle-class women. It argues that they were excluded from the world of work at the beginning of the nineteenth century but had made some gains by the end. The occupations deemed suitable for middle-class women tended to be those which accorded perfectly with their role as wife and mother. For instance, the governess and the teacher both cared for children.

b) Women's work changed for two main reasons. Firstly, feminist pressure demanded greater challenges. Secondly, changes in technology opened up further opportunities.

Answering an essay question on *'Women and Work'*

1 The impact of industrialisation on women's employment was more varied and far less dramatic than the standard image of the mill girl implies. (Tilly and Scott) Discuss.

This is an example of a wide-ranging essay which expects you to understand the broad sweep of women's work in the nineteenth century and to realise that women's work encompassed infinitely more than factory work. However, examiners are often impressed by candidates who challenge the question so you might like to examine the effect of

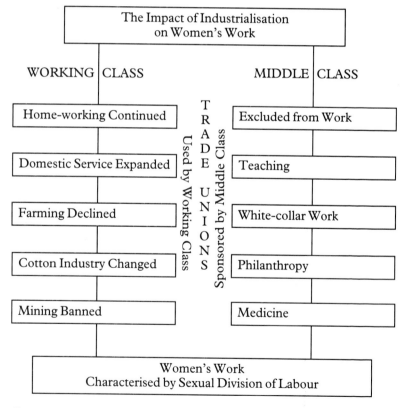

Summary - Women and Work

industrialisation on cotton workers as well. This quote also seems to suggest that working-class women were the only groups who worked! Therefore, you might allude to the variety of women's work during industrialisation before demonstrating that domestic service was the most typical occupation of the young female. Although industrialisation affected everyone, even if only indirectly, it was not always that dramatic as large numbers of women continued in their usual work. Women's work both before, during and after industrialisation was characterised by low pay, long hours and poor working conditions and tended to be associated with domesticity.

Source-based questions on 'Women and Work'

1 The Census
Read the extract from the census abstracts on page 48. Answer the following questions. Bear in mind that census returns were unreliable in recording women's work. Women often worked in seasonal jobs so were not at work when the census enumerator called. Similarly, married women's work often went unrecorded unless they were head of household.
a) Which occupations employed the most and the least women? (1 mark)
b) What does the answer to the above tell you about the status, type and nature of women's work? (5 marks)
c) Given the weakness of the census as evidence are these findings of any value? (3 marks)

2 Domestic Service
Read the extract about domestic service on page 53. Answer the following questions. (Hannah Cullwick wrote this extract. She was secretly married to an upper-middle-class barrister and poet called Arthur Munby who liked Hannah Cullwick to dress up in servant's clothes. Sometimes she dressed up as a slave for Arthur Munby. Hannah Cullwick was expected to write a diary every day for him to read.)
a) Write this diary extract in modern English. (2 marks)
b) Given the nature of this evidence, is it of any use to an historian researching the life of domestic servants? (3 marks)

CHAPTER 5

Prostitution and its Repression

Prostitution caused great concern in Victorian and Edwardian Britain. In 1860 there were apparently 25,000 prostitutes in London alone. Considered a 'social evil', prostitution commanded attention from the Church, the State, philanthropists, feminists and others, each of which held different perspectives on the causes of prostitution and offered a range of solutions to control, regulate and ultimately to end it. Penitentiaries and Asylums were founded to reform individual prostitutes, the Contagious Diseases Acts were passed to make paid sex safe for the armed forces and preventive organisations were set up to tackle the underlying causes of prostitution.

Historians generally agree that prostitution was founded on the biting poverty of working-class women and tend to agree that there was a direct causal relationship between the low level of women's wages and female prostitution. Certainly, prostitutes seemed to be recruited from poorly paid occupations more easily than from others. Dressmakers, seamstresses, milliners, bonnet makers, agricultural labourers, barmaids and above all domestic servants were vulnerable to the lure of the streets. These occupations were characterised either by intermittent seasonal unemployment or low wages and sometimes both. Even in prosperous times, it was difficult for these working-class women to live on their meagre wages, let alone save towards leaner times. For many, prostitution was a part-time job, taken to supplement their income or to tide them over when unemployed.

Women's opportunity for financial independence was further jeopardised when the Poor Law Amendment Act of 1834 attempted to abolish outdoor relief making the workhouse a grim alternative to destitution. Workhouses allegedly proved to be excellent recruitment centres for prostitution because sexually innocent young women not only mixed indiscriminately with prostitutes but workhouses discharged young women into domestic service. Women employed as servants were considered the most susceptible to prostitution: one Salvation Army register showed that as many as 88 per cent of reclaimed prostitutes had been former domestic servants.

Poverty may have been the overwhelming reason for prostitution but, according to some historians, inadequate wages did not necessarily drive women onto the streets. Some sweated workers, such as matchbox makers and fur pullers, tended not to become prostitutes however low their wages might sink. Women who were extremely poor were generally not driven to prostitution unless they were homeless and without family or friends. It is impossible to know, but some historians believe that prostitutes chose their profession because they wanted more money than their low-paid work could provide. It has been argued by historians that prostitutes had a wild impulsive nature, a restlessness and a need for

Sorrow, *a drawing by Van Gogh, 1882*

independence which drove them on to the streets in order to gain those commodities valued by the newly created consumer society.

Evidence from contemporary records indicates that cruel, drunken and uncaring parents, or step-parents sometimes forced young girls to leave home. Overcrowded homes were considered to be breeding grounds for incest as families lived in one room with several people sharing a bed. Uncles slept with nieces, brothers with sisters, cousins with cousins which opened up great possibility of sexual abuse.

Consequently, one is led to believe that it is inadequate to argue that economic factors provided the only reason for prostitution. Lack of money was certainly a strong motivating factor for many destitute women but other, more personal and social, reasons also played an important role. Students reading this book might disagree with many of the reasons put forward by the nineteenth-century commentator, William Ryan, outlined below, but at least he goes beyond a simplistic economic explanation:

1 Causes of prostitution - seduction; neglect of parents; idleness; the
  low price of needle and other female work; the employment of
  young men milliners and drapers in shops in place of women; the
  facilities of prostitution; prevalence of intemperance; music and
5 dancing in public houses, saloons and theatres; the impression that
  males are not equally culpable as females; female love of dress and
  of superior society; the seductive promises of men; the idea that
  prostitution is indispensable, poverty; want of education;
  ignorance; misery; innate licentiousness; improper prints, books
10 and obscene weekly publications; and the profligacy of modern
  civilisation.

1 Reforming Prostitutes

Historians tend to acknowledge that the penitentiary system of reform, inspired by the Church of England, was the hallmark of late eighteenth- and nineteenth-century Britain. Indeed, penitentiaries and asylums can be considered as part of a Christian 'archipelago' of reform which stretched all over the British Isles. The first penitentiary opened in London in 1758 stated that it accepted all women except those who were black. Its 'success' led to the establishment of other institutions. In 1807 the London Female Penitentiary was established at Pentonville. In 1849 Mariquita Tennant offered asylum to prostitutes at the Clewer House of Mercy near Windsor, which was later extended by the Sisters of St John the Baptist. Others followed suit. The Church Penitentiary Association was established in 1852 to co-ordinate and promote this reform movement. Scotland and Ireland also favoured the penitential system and built similar institutions to those in England.

Recent research by feminist historians, who have examined reform institutions in England, Ireland and Scotland, suggests that the attitudes of asylum managers towards prostitutes were informed by a set of gender, class and religious assumptions. Prostitution was seen as a full-time female profession: male prostitution was never discussed or considered. It was also considered a female problem for it was only prostitutes, not the men who bought their sexual favours, who were the objects of moral scrutiny. Illicit sex, one can assume, was considered to be a natural biological urge for men but not for women. Prostitutes were perceived as sexual contaminators and a dangerous role model for single women because they challenged the notion of the sexually passive woman - women were expected to be either virgins or wives who succumbed, a little unwillingly, to male advances. Prostitutes, as sexualised women, undermined this principle of female propriety and posed a threat to the institution of marriage, the sanctity of the family and ultimately the sexual and moral order of the time. It was feared that female prostitution affected and contaminated the whole of society, ruined health, destroyed spiritual life, undermined mental power and ate, like a cancer, at the heart of British life. Prostitution was seen to tarnish the minds of the innocent as 'it flaunts about the streets, it meets our sons and our daughters, and it taints the atmosphere in which it moves.'

Prostitution was held to be a grievous sin by the Church of England, with prostitutes considered as sinners who would be excluded from the Kingdom of Heaven and condemned to ever-lasting fire. Parallels were drawn between prostitution and Sodom and Gomorrah. The language and the sentiments expressed by the Church of England convey images of sin, damnation and a punitive God. Most of the language was resonant with religious fervour and the redemptive power of God, as this extract from an asylum report demonstrates:

1 It is a sin for which signal punishment was, with the marked approval of God, summarily inflicted under the Law. It is a sin which, in part, drew down upon Sodom and Gomorrah, brimstone and fire from the Lord out of heaven. It is a sin which leadeth unto
5 'death'. It is a sin which God will especially judge. It is a sin which will cause its impenitent perpetrators to be excluded from the Kingdom of God. It is a sin for the sake of which the wrath of God cometh on the children of disobedience... It is a sin which only those who are without right understanding indulge in. It is a sin
10 from which persons are exhorted to flee as from a pestilence.

Even the name that the Roman Catholic Church in Ireland, the Church of England and the Episcopelian Church in Scotland gave to their reform institutions, Magdalen asylums, evoked images of penitence - women entered an institution blessed with the name of that most famous of sinners. And like Mary Magdalen, inmates were encouraged to repent their past life, ask forgiveness for their sins and make a fresh start so that they could be assured entry to future Paradise.

Not surprisingly, given these attitudes, reform institutions were punitive. Historians agree that penitentiaries shared a great deal in common, whatever their geographical location. Once accepted into the institution, young women were remolded into a more pleasing feminised working-class model. They were compelled to stay for at least two years, had their hair cropped and wore a special regulatory uniform which was quickly identifiable. People in York, for instance, easily recognised penitentiary inmates by their grey cloaks and bonnets. On entry to the institution, freedom was completely curtailed. Inmates were denied access to the ordinary daily pattern of life: they could not shop, visit friends or go for a leisurely walk unaccompanied. They were forbidden to go out alone and were either denied contact with friends and family or allowed to see them only at strictly regulated intervals. Letters were inspected by the supervisor in charge. At the end of each day inmates were shut away in dormitories where beds were often packed close together. It was a self-contained social world where the only contact with the outside world was through the staff. This isolation was popular with the managers of these institutions because they believed that inmates might internalise the cultural values of the penitentiary more easily if they were not distracted by corrupt outside influences.

Discipline was strict and life in each institution well regulated. Snuff, swearing, and fighting were banned, as was talking about one's past. In the home at Clewer, near Windsor, inmates were taught to bow low before the nuns who managed the institution and to speak only when spoken to. Decisions were made for the inmates not by them. From the time they got up in the morning to the time they went to bed at night the lives of the inmates were regulated like those of children. For two years, the women were rarely alone. Like the inmates of prisons or convents they lived, worked and prayed alongside others: it was an enforced communal existence.

Historians acknowledge that in order to maintain discipline and keep the institution financially viable, all inmates had to work. Occupations in such institutions ranged from weaving carpets, making lace, toys, gloves and artificial flowers but most inmates worked in the laundry. In York, as in most other institutions, the Assistant Matron taught the inmates how to wash, starch and iron in order for them to become laundry maids in the outside world. Indeed, laundry work was the leitmotif of these type of institutions. Laundry work helped cut the cost of food, clothing and confinement. Charitable donations contributed about two-thirds of the cost of these institutions so laundry work was often an important part of the annual revenue. The famous public school at Eton, for example, paid the Clewer House of Mercy £270 per annum to wash the household linen and personal laundry of 70 boys.

Some feminists have argued that laundry work reinforced class and gender conformity by preparing the inmate for working-class female work. Laundry work trained inmates for the lowliest type of domestic service which was viewed as the most fitting occupation for working-class women. No opportunity was ever given for young female inmates to transcend either their class background or their gender role. Increased job opportunities, particularly in the latter part of the century, opened up employment prospects for women generally but training other than laundry was never offered by reform institutions.

Laundry work was chosen for religious as well as economic reasons. Cleanliness was the grand metaphor of religious purity - after all cleanliness was supposedly next to godliness. In eliminating physical dirt, order was also to be established in the spiritual world of the inmates. It was also the metaphor of absolution. In scrubbing sheets white as the purest snow, inmates washed away their sins and regained their shining soul. In addition, laundry work may have been favoured because hard physical labour acted as a penance. In working hard, in primitive conditions, inmates atoned for their sins. Certainly, laundry work was very harsh. One historian has commented on the fact that workers suffered from rheumatism, ulcerated legs, bronchitis and other allied complaints as a result of standing for long hours in ill-ventilated damp rooms.

Magdalen asylums were not always successful in promoting compliance. Historians claim that many of the institutions had difficulty in coping with the inmates who quarrelled with one another, refused to work, stole, told lies and were rude to the matrons. Inmates often wanted to leave but it was not always easy to do so; they were interviewed by the matron and frequently put in solitary confinement to think it over. Rather than submit to this treatment, many ran away. Inmates at York, Glasgow and Windsor squeezed through windows to escape over walls to the street below. Those who dared to run away were sometimes charged with theft of their uniform and sentenced to periods of imprisonment.

However, the research carried out so far on reform, has been based on the military town of Windsor, the Nonconformist city of Birmingham, the cathedral city of York, the largely Presbyterian cities of Glasgow and Edinburgh and the Catholic country of Ireland, so it is difficult to establish whether this method of reform applied elsewhere in Britain.

2 The Contagious Diseases Acts 1864-6

In 1870 Catherine Pickles, a young girl of sixteen, was suspected of being a common prostitute, arrested by military police, taken to hospital and forcibly examined for venereal disease. Catherine protested at this treatment but no one listened - it was the law. Six years previously the British government had passed the first of a series of Contagious

Diseases Acts which gave the police powers to arrest women suspected of being a 'common prostitute'. Once apprehended, women were ordered to undergo an internal examination at a certified hospital. Women, like Catherine Pickles, were roughly treated in these places. Internal examinations were conducted by doctors who were neither gentle nor particularly hygienic, often in rooms which were not properly screened. Examinations rarely lasted more than a minute: one doctor in Plymouth examined 70 women a day! Catherine Pickles, like so many falsely accused women, was found to be healthy and set free but without an apology. But if found diseased, she could have been detained for treatment up to a period of three months or until she was pronounced cured. Treatment was neither pleasant nor effective: mercury, a highly toxic substance, was the only medical remedy available.

The Contagious Diseases Acts of 1864, 1866 and 1869 applied to garrison towns and naval ports such as Portsmouth, Plymouth, Woolwich, Chatham, Sheerness, Aldershot, Colchester, Shorncliffe, the Curragh, Cork and Queenstown. The first of these Acts was never publicly debated in the House of Commons and was passed in silence without a division. Most of the important stages of the Bill occurred at the end of the evening when only about 50 exhausted and sleepy MPs were present. Some even assumed that they had passed an animals bill as previous bills had applied to the control of infectious diseases such as foot and mouth. However, this Act applied to women only: it was to stop the spread of venereal disease.

a) Why the Contagious Diseases Acts were Passed

Great concern was expressed over the health of the armed forces at this time. The three great diseases of the eighteenth century - fever, flux and scurvy - had been controlled, leaving venereal disease as the major infectious disease threatening the armed forces. For a long time, the military authorities had accepted a high incidence of venereal disease among the (mainly bachelor) troops, but this attitude had changed with the onset of the Crimean War in 1854. The considerable death rate of soldiers due to all types of sickness convinced both the general public and the authorities of the importance of a fit army.

This was confirmed by the statistics of the Army Medical Department, which showed that the sanitary reforms which had taken place had reduced nearly every illness save that of venereal disease. In 1858 the Report of the Royal Commission on the Sanitary State of the Army, (which concentrated on factors such as the state of the barracks, unsuitable uniforms and the unhealthy life styles of soldiers) registered concern over debauchery in the armed forces:

1 A soldier is a man who, as a rule, is unmarried, he has an immense

amount of time hanging heavily on his hands, his duties are brief, and he has no recreation to take the place of regular occupation. He is generally quartered in London or some large provincial town, 5 with every facility for dissipation; while his only substitute for a home is a pestilential barrack-room, in which he sleeps by night and eats by day. It is no wonder that he is driven to debauchery.

By 1864 venereal disease was responsible for one out of every three sick cases in the army. Ships docked in Portsmouth harbour with a full complement of sailors were often incapable of sailing a few weeks later because of a high infection rate. Loss of man hours in the armed forces was therefore a crucial factor in the debate about regulating prostitutes. If paid sex was made safer for the military, a fit fighting force would be more likely.

Military men fully supported the CDAs because they believed that there was less venereal disease in colonised countries. It was thought that the low incidence of venereal disease was because prostitutes in the colonised countries of India, Malta, Hong Kong, Aden and Gibraltar were all compulsorily medically examined on a regular basis. It was believed that Malta had virtually eliminated venereal disease because of a strongly enforced regulatory system. Colonial precedents certainly shaped the legislation in England: the CDAs' protection of the armed forces, their administration by plain clothes police and the assumption that prostitutes were a recognisable group all derived from colonial practice.

The medical profession in general and the influential doctor William Acton, in particular helped shape public opinion in support of the CDAs. William Acton was a well-known expert on venereal disease who had studied the regulatory system in Paris and whose publication of a book titled *Prostitution* prompted a debate about regulation. In the first edition of his book, Acton claimed that venereal disease threatened to weaken the British population if it remained unchecked and advocated the regulation of the prostitute. He supported the CDAs wholeheartedly because of a belief that the Acts lessened the danger of infection by the prostitute to her client. Acton said to prostitutes 'You cannot be prevented from following this sad career which you have chosen; we cannot force you to abstain from vice; but we can and will take care that your shameful lives shall no longer work injury to the health of others, or outrage public decency.'

According to some historians, the erosion of *laissez faire* contributed to creating an atmosphere in which intervention was possible. Government, it is said, was more willing to intervene in the lives of its citizens by the 1860s than it had in previous decades. Chadwick's Public Health Act of 1848, along with the compulsory smallpox vaccination of all new babies in 1853, had shown the effect of medical pressure and legislative reform upon the health of the nation. Prostitutes were seen as a similar public nuisance to sewage: they should be cleaned, sanitised and made safe for the general public in the same manner as fetid drains. Thus John Liddell, in the Report of the Committee upon Venereal Disease in the Army and Navy, could argue that:

1 sewers ... decayed meat, etc; ... the time seems very favourable for trying to get the legislature to place these women under the immediate surveillance of the police and to commit them compulsorily, when diseased, to Lock wards prepared for their
5 cure. ... Surely it would not be difficult to get a rider to the Health of Towns Act, to which I think the public would agree, charging the police with the control of those women; investing them with the power to inform against and cause to be medically examined those women who are suspected to be diseased, who should be
10 committed to a hospital and detained there until cured.

Both protective legislation and the CDAs can be seen as part of a process of regulating women. Factory legislation, for example, had eroded women's contractual power by reducing the number of hours that could be worked. In the same way the CDAs weakened women's position in the sexual market by submitting them to possible arrest and detention, thus denying them the opportunity to work.

Finally, it has been observed that the Contagious Diseases Acts were a clear example of the double standard of Victorian morality whereby it was more defensible for a man to engage in non-marital sex but highly sinful for a woman. In *Prostitution and Victorian Society* Judith Walkowitz argues that the CDAs were consistent with a set of attitudes towards women, sexuality and class that permeated Victorian society. The CDAs, she believes, represented the officially sanctioned double standard of morality which tried to separate women into whores and virgins. Concern was expressed by the government because it wished to ensure that prostitutes were clean and wholesome for their customers and remained indifferent as to whether the customers passed on diseases to the prostitutes. The CDAs were brought in because the government believed that the male use of prostitutes was a dangerous sexual activity which needed to be made safe. Indeed, Walkowitz has even viewed the CDAs as a class-based piece of legislation because the Acts tended to apply to working-class street-walkers rather than courtesans or those who worked in high-class brothels.

Superficially, the Acts appeared to diminish the incidence of disease in the restricted towns but the numbers who contracted venereal disease probably fell for other reasons. Rather than be arrested, registered and confined to hospital, prostitutes simply left these towns to work elsewhere, or lived outside the restricted area and travelled in daily. In Maidstone 91 women were registered as prostitutes in 1866 but by 1870 50 per cent had left the district. The Acts may well have improved the health of the towns to which they applied but they damaged that of neighbouring towns as prostitutes simply moved to unregulated areas.

b) Why the Contagious Diseases Acts were Repealed

Eventually, after years of campaigning, the CDAs were repealed in 1886. Josephine Butler, leader of the Ladies National Association, (LNA) was once viewed by historians as the most important figure in the repeal movement but this perception has been revised. The significance of regional campaigns and the political influence of sympathetic MPs were to be of equal importance in repealing the CDAs as Josephine Butler's highly public profile. Nonetheless, there is no doubting Josephine Butler's considerable importance in the repeal movement. Married to a Church of England clergyman, she seemed the ideal candidate to lead the crusade against the CDAs. *The campaign she led began in December 1869 when the* Daily News published the 'Women's Protest' against the Acts signed by Harriet Martineau, Florence Nightingale, Josephine Butler and more than a hundred other women. The publication of this manifesto was a sensation, it was reprinted and discussed widely. From that moment on, Josephine Butler strove energetically to publicise the repeal movement. In her first year she travelled an exhausting 3,700 miles to 99 meetings. Said to be a brilliant speaker, she allegedly captivated even the opposition by her charismatic appeal and hard-hitting speeches.

Josephine Butler, and the LNA she headed, certainly used persuasive arguments against the CDAs. Objections were voiced by the LNA that prostitutes were punished for the conveyance of the disease rather then the men who used them. Female victims, Butler argued, were humiliated by a degrading examination with a 'steel penis' (soon dubbed instrumental rape). The following quote by a prostitute was used by Josephine Butler in her speeches to demonstrate the injustice of the CDAs:

1 It is men, men, only men, from the first to the last that we have to
do with! To please a man I did wrong, at first, then I was flung
about from man to man. Men police lay hands on us. By men we
are examined, doctored and messed on with. In the hospital it is a
5 man again who makes prayers and reads the Bible for us. We are
had up before magistrates who are men, and we never get out of the
hands of men until we die.

Repealers believed that making women responsible for the carrying of venereal disease merely reinforced the sexual double standard rather than stopping venereal disease. Repressive legislation, it was alleged, could not halt the spread of venereal disease because men still contaminated their innocent wives. It was also claimed that the Acts legalised prostitution because legislation encouraged safe, paid sex rather than its elimination. Vice increased its attraction because it ceased to be hazardous which contributed, in the reformers' minds, to the growth of evil. Some were concerned about the infringement of civil liberties because the CDAs violated the rights of the individual, allowed State interference in personal affairs, increased central government authority and gave police greater powers of arrest. Finally, the CDAs were seen to be a class piece of legislation because they affected street-walkers or common prostitutes rather than upper-class courtesans.

Petitions, deputations, lobbies, meetings, leaflets and articles - typical middle-class campaigning strategies - were all used to rally support. Petitioning was used widely because it was the only constitutional means by which women, who were unable to vote, could influence Parliament. Over 18,000 petitions, signed by 2,657,348 people, were presented to Parliament between 1870-86. Pressure was put on prospective MPs campaigning in their constituencies, and sympathetic MPs were pressurised to keep the campaign in parliamentary focus. The LNA urged the adoption of MPs sympathetic to repeal politics and canvassed against those who were antagonistic. For example, as a result of LNA interference, the Liberal Sir Henry Storks was defeated in Colchester 1870 and the First Lord of the Admiralty, H.C.E. Childers, had his majority dramatically reduced from 233 to 80 in a bye-election. Meetings were used to drum up support and to spread the repeal message. Separate meetings of men and women were often convened as a way of avoiding the criticism that discussion of sexual topics was inappropriate for mixed audiences. Annual meetings which lasted one or two days were used as rallying points for the members. The *Shield* newspaper, the journal of the LNA, informed, recruited and persuaded many people to see the justice of repeal and publicised the work of the local associations. It also drew attention to individual women persecuted by the CDAs. For example, the suicide of Mrs Percy, a professional singer and actress, who had lost her reputation and her job when she was accused of prostitution, provided the repeal movement with its first martyr and acted as a catalyst for pressure.

The publicity generated by the LNA was not always positive and its election tactics were met with hostility in some districts. In Colchester, opponents threw refuse and furniture at the repealers and threatened to burn down the hotel where Josephine Butler was staying. On many occasions the female campaigners were accused of dabbling in filth because they discussed sexual issues. One MP even thought that middle- class female repealers were worse than prostitutes because they should have known better.

Josephine Butler and the LNA did not campaign alone. They received support from a variety of individuals and groups who were equally determined to get rid of the CDAs. Daniel Cooper, Secretary of the Society for the Rescue of Young Women and Children, was one of the first to campaign against further legislation but not until the influential National Association for the Promotion of Social Science denounced the Acts did a repeal movement emerge. As a result of its commitment to repeal, the National Anti-Contagious Disease Acts Extension Association, later known as the National Association, was formed to protest against the extension of the Acts. Local repeal groups also proliferated between 1870 and 1886. The Birmingham and Nottingham Associations for Repeal (which later became the Midland Counties Electoral Union), the Northern Counties League for Repeal, the National Medical Association, the Friends Association for Repeal, and the Working Men's National League, which were founded at this time, all formed part of the national movement for repeal. In addition, at least one historian has argued that Henry Wilson, leader of the northern campaigns, has been neglected in favour of Josephine Butler. It has been claimed that Wilson was an 'organisational genius' whose cultivation of the Liberal Party was invaluable to the repeal movement. Working backstage without the glamour of Butler's crusade, Wilson was a workhorse who provided the backbone to the campaign waged by the LNA and deserves as much credit as Butler in the successful repeal of the CDAs.

Without financial and moral support from powerful individuals and organisations, the repeal movement might have floundered. The various repeal groups received a great deal of money from Nonconformists and eventually gained support from influential men in the trade union movement and the medical profession, all of which encouraged Parliament to take their cause seriously. Substantial sums of money were donated, particularly by wealthy Quakers, to the various associations which enabled the repeal groups to launch and continue their publicity campaigns. By the 1880s the Trades Union Congress had condemned the CDAs with influential trade union leaders such as Joseph Arch, Henry Broadhurst and William Lovett all advocating repeal. In 1874 an important pressure group, the National Medical Association for Repeal, was founded which convinced a number of doctors of the need for action against the CDAs.

Parliamentary support was obviously essential to overturn the CDAs but neither the Liberals nor the Tories initially supported repeal: other issues such as Ireland, imperialism, suffrage, religion, urbanisation and education were amongst their most urgent concerns. Throughout the 1870s individual MPs introduced private members repeal bills into the House of Commons but, because they did not have party support, received only a minority vote. Successive governments examined the issue but tended to favour extension rather than repeal: a Royal Commission appointed in 1871 reported in favour not only of the continuation of the CDAs but of their extension, stating 'there is no comparison to be made between the prostitute and the men who consort with them. With the one sex the offence is committed as a matter of gain; with the other it is the irregular indulgence of a natural impulse.' Luckily, for the repealers, the Government did not implement the Commission's recommendations.

By the mid 1870s Liberal support was growing. The First Lord of the Admiralty, Childers (who had once been an advocate of the Acts), Gladstone (who had once voted for them), Bright and Forster all supported repeal. When the Liberal government lost the general election in 1874 it seemed as if the impetus for repeal would disappear. However, the fall of Gladstone's government freed an influential repealer, James Stansfeld, from the responsibilities of office and enabled him to focus on the repeal campaign. Stansfeld, a Unitarian brewer and leading republican radical supported feminist causes but did not wish to lead the movement because of party-political loyalty which was initially in favour of the CDAs. His support proved to be a turning point in the campaign. When James Stansfeld spoke out in favour of repeal the press took notice. He was said to bring two valuable gifts to the repeal movement - prestige and political experience. As a result he attracted considerable support from the clergy and medical men, and as Josephine Butler's private adviser he was able to mediate between her and Gladstone.

Eventually, the increased support for repeal encouraged the Conservative government under Disraeli to examine the practice of the CDAs once again. A Select Committee of MPs, which sat between 1879 and 1882, was formed but largely because the Conservatives lost the general election of 1880, the membership of this Committee changed. To the repealers' delight, Stansfeld was appointed to the Select Committee to ensure that the newly elected Liberal government's voice was heard. Even so, it was impossible to obtain a unanimous verdict so both a majority and minority report were submitted. Although the majority recommended the continuation of the Acts, Stansfeld lent his support to the minority document. With renewed confidence the repealers launched their last attack. On 12 April 1883 the National Liberal Federation passed a repeal resolution and just over a week later Stansfeld moved a successful resolution in Parliament that 'This House disapproves of the compulsory examination of women under the Contagious Diseases Acts'. This in effect made the CDAs unworkable. Three years later, after many bills, a Commission, a Select Committee and insistent campaigning the Repeal Bill of March 1886, like the CDAs before it, was passed without a division. But it had taken 22 years to succeed.

3 Preventing Prostitution

a) Ladies' Associations

Prevention was seen to be better than cure. Ellice Hopkins, whom historians are unanimous was crucial in the development of preventive work, said that 'A fence at the top of a cliff is better than an ambulance at the bottom'. Largely through the efforts of Ellice Hopkins, Ladies' Associations for the Care of Friendless Girls (Ladies' Associations) were set up in towns and cities across the country. Associations were established in Birmingham, Bristol, Nottingham, London, Edinburgh, Torquay, Cheltenham, Southampton, Winchester, Bradford, Dundee and Perth, and subsequently in other towns. By 1885 there were 85 such organisations catering for predominately working-class young women. Each organisation was divided into four sections: a preventive branch which had a training home for domestic servants and a free registry office and clothing club for them; an educational branch; a workhouse Magdalen branch; and lastly a petitioning branch.

Unlike the reform movement, the preventive movement was founded and managed by middle-class women. Visions of female solidarity had prompted some women to engage in this type of philanthropic work. Very many women who promoted the preventive movement were involved in the suffrage movement or other feminist struggles. To some extent women's rights and moral reform were, if not inextricably linked, then certainly intimately connected. Feminism provided the justification for women who wished to participate in moral reform politics and the Ladies' Association aimed to unite working-class and middle-class women. However, the woman-centred approach of the Ladies' Association existed within a frame of power and authority. Female unity was seen in, if not paternalistic ways, then certainly maternalistic ones, exhibiting the familiar mixture of humanitarianism and class domination. It was a one-way power relationship whereby middle-class women implemented their own definition of what were considered to be correct forms of behaviour and appropriated the morality of the working class. Equally this care was framed within an economic context as only those thought to be 'deserving' of financial assistance were helped.

Training homes were founded to train young girls how to be domestic servants and registry offices were set up to find jobs for them. Domestic service training homes were institutions, like the reform homes, which provided working-class young women with the opportunity to train for work that was distinctly working-class. They were yet another mechanism whereby selected young women were educated into the social mores of the middle-class community - they were taught to be polite, charming and chaste - but without accruing the economic benefits of such a shift. At no time did the Ladies' Associations offer to extend equal work opportunities to the inmate even though some of the middle-class women involved were not impervious to current debates about female emancipation. Alternatives to domestic service were therefore never offered because young working-class women were expected to remain as lowly paid workers rather than aspire to the jobs of the male skilled working class or indeed the middle class.

Educational branches saw themselves as the ideological wing of the

Ladies' Associations. They wanted to attack the causes of immorality at a fundamental level by creating the context in which moral values could thrive. Ladies' Associations set up groups such as the Snowdrop Bands to encourage chastity and modesty amongst young working-class girls. Each young woman who joined a Snowdrop Band was issued with a membership card on which a picture of a snowdrop was drawn as an artistic metaphor of purity. On the back of each card was printed a promise which encapsulated the aims of the Snowdrop Bands:

1 We the Members of the Snowdrop Band, sign our names to show that we have agreed that wherever we are, and in whatever company, we will, with God's help, earnestly try, both by our example and influence to discourage all wrong conversation, light
5 and immodest conduct, and the reading of foolish and bad books.

However, the impetus for Snowdrop Bands originated in a philosophy that was damning of the working class. Concern was expressed by one Snowdrop Band leader of 'the fearfully low tone of conversation which generally prevails when any number of uneducated women are thrown together' which was hardly supportive of the class harmony promulgated by the Ladies' Associations.

The Ladies' Associations also visited single mothers in workhouses and helped them to find work. Unmarried mothers were at one and the same time viewed benevolently and as an economic drain on the rates. Single mothers were categorised into the deserving and the undeserving poor. The Ladies' Associations created moral hierarchies by differentiating between those who were thought worthy of help and those who were not. They believed in the classification of the inmates and the separation of what was perceived the hardened and the depraved from the younger and more innocent. A distinction was made between those who had led a life of 'professional vice' and those who had been led astray, but only once, by promises, ignorance or childish folly. Only single women in their first illegitimate confinement were visited and helped. Financial considerations were also important when help was eventually given. The Ladies' Association aimed to find work for the mother in order to discourage them from being a burden on the rates. They also encouraged mothers to apply for affiliation summonses to force the father to pay towards the cost of his illegitimate offspring. The Ladies' Association was concerned that men, not just women, should be held responsible for the child. However, the reason that fathers were held equally responsible for an illegitimate baby had as much do with economics as with morality for the Ladies' Association were again conscious of the demand on ratepayers.

The Ladies' Association subscribed to the 'slippery slope' theory whereby single motherhood led directly to prostitution. It was feared that single parenthood prefaced a move to 'the ranks of the only trade that opens its arms to a helpless, ill-trained, homeless woman, burdened with a child, and with the stigma of the workhouse upon her character'. Indeed, it was widely held that the workhouse maternity wards were peopled by prostitutes. In helping single mothers, the Ladies' Association believed that it had stopped the moral degeneration of the nation by stopping prostitution at source. Unmarried mothers - whether they became prostitutes or not - also posed a threat to the social equilibrium. Marriage, home and family were seen as the bedrock of Western civilisation and of order, stability and morality within the country. Unmarried pregnant women were the living embodiment of immorality and an all too visible reminder of what was termed sexual incontinence. In addition, single women challenged the middle-class construction of femininity. In the nineteenth century marriage was a major signifier in constructing femininity but single mothers under-mined this equation and offered an alternative definition of woman.

Feminists may have promoted an idealised picture of female solidarity but it was undermined in distinct ways by class. There was little or no unity between benefactor and beneficiary for middle-class women shared little community of interest with the working class. Time after time, working-class women were categorised into the deserving and undeserving, a division consonant with the class ideology of Victorian and Edwardian Britain.

b) Social Purity

By the 1880s, feminists held that men were equally responsible as women for the continuance of prostitution. It was believed that prostitution could be eliminated only if single men became celibate and married men remained faithful to their wives. In addition, it was thought necessary to create a moral climate in Britain. Social purity movements were founded to achieve this. Many different, disparate societies were formed to eliminate prostitution and to encourage moral behaviour but these groups are not easy to categorise as they varied greatly in their nature, methods and organisation and appealed to different classes. Social purity groups were at one and the same time progressive and conservative. Although they were sympathetic to the penitent fallen woman they ruthlessly cracked down upon those who continued to act immorally.

One such group was the Church of England Purity Society which worked alongside the White Cross Army. Ellice Hopkins helped to found both and they merged in 1891 to remain the Church's organisation for work among men until 1939. Both of these organisations criticised sexual incontinence and emphasised the importance of purity for men. For 5 shillings' subscription men over the age of 18 could join a diocesan branch of CEPS in order to inspire 'Purity amongst men, A chivalrous respect for womanhood, Preservation of the young from contamination, Rescue work, and a higher tone of public opinion.' Despite the hard work of the organisers this group failed to recruit enough upper-class men to make it viable. While the CEPS attracted the upper echelons of society, the White Cross Army aimed to recruit working-class males. Much of its success can be attributed to Ellice Hopkins who spent 21 years of her life working for the organisation.

In this time she addressed hundreds of meetings and wrote most of the pamphlets, which sold over two million copies in the USA and Britain. Hopkins spoke and wrote eloquently and simply of how poor girls were exploited by procurers and encouraged working-class men to act as modern Galahads by rescuing women from dens of iniquity, refusing to consort with prostitutes and persuading other men to live pure lives. Branches of the White Cross were formed in the army, the navy and in local dioceses in Britain and the rest of the world. Africa, America, Australia, Canada, China, Jamaica, Japan, Trinidad and New Zealand all had thriving branches putting forward the same message:

1. To treat all women with respect, and endeavour to protect them from wrong and degradation
2. To endeavour to put down all indecent language and coarse jests
3. To maintain the law of purity as equally binding upon men and women
4. To endeavour to spread these principles among my companions, and to try to help my younger brothers
5. To use every possible means to fulfil the command 'Keep thyself pure'.

Largely as a result of social purity campaigns a Criminal Law Amendment Act (CLAA) was passed in 1885 which raised the age of sexual consent to 16, gave police greater powers to close down brothels and made male homosexuality illegal. The National Vigilance Association was formed in the same year to help enforce the CLAA. Between 1885 and 1914 the NVA sought to question, challenge, curtail and change male sexual behaviour as well as women's. It was a complex mixture of progressive and reactionary politics. On the one hand the NVA had a strong commitment to feminism (usually viewed as a progressive movement) while on the other hand it wanted to give the police greater powers of arrest (usually viewed as a reactionary idea). The NVA dealt with any subject connected to what was perceived to be the moral wellbeing of the nation. These ranged from the suppression of obscene literature, indecent pictures and photographs, indecent advertising of brothels, child abuse, the employment of children on the stage and semi-nudity in music halls.

Obscene literature and indecent advertising were linked, in the NVA's mind, with moral turpitude so they tried to ban them. The NVA campaigned for legislation such as the Indecent Advertisement Act of 1889 and even persuaded a reluctant New Scotland Yard to establish a department to deal with indecent literature. The Birmingham branch successfully prosecuted men who produced and sold improper prints, made immodest speeches, posted indecent advertisements or sold objectionable Christmas cards. Exposure to such literature, it was believed, encouraged 'sexual incontinence' and augmented the pervasive corruption of the day because it created the climate in which immorality thrived. Indecent advertisements, for example, were blamed for inciting immoral thoughts in the minds of the impressionable young and this in turn led to immoral actions. There was decisive proof, according to the NVA, that immoral literature and advertising encouraged licentious behaviour. According to the NVA there was a definite link between language and action: indecent literature fostered indecent behaviour. The NVA believed that words, as well as deeds, undermined morality. Its advocacy of a robust prosecution policy was based on the damage that immoral literature posed to the general public and it was considered inappropriate for anybody, not just the vulnerable, to see and read it. Indecent literature, it was believed, should be banned outright. There was never any debate about the freedom and rights of citizens to determine their own sexuality or to choose as freely consenting adults. In addition, there was an agreed definition, never publicly stated, about what constituted indecent literature. The NVA made no distinction between pornography (which can debase people) and informative sexual literature (which can benefit people). All sexual literature was condemned as highly indecent. Any public portrayal of sexuality was deemed to be degrading to humanity so educational leaflets, erotica and pornography were condemned equally and ultimately censored.

Part of the work of the NVA embraced the suppression of the white slave trade. It persuaded several European countries, and after the First World War, the League of Nations, to try to stop the traffic in young girls. The NVA was sympathetic to young women who had been unwilling victims in this type of seduction but viewed those unrepentant much more severely. Prostitutes who wished to continue working were treated harshly and excluded from the category of the deserving. In engaging in prostitution women allegedly defied the concept of femininity, violated their gender role and relinquished their rights to the care and protection usually extended to the 'weaker' sex. Whereas repentant prostitutes were cared for, the unrepentant needed to be restrained. Consequently the working prostitute's freedom was curbed when the NVA used the newly passed CLAA to close down brothels. The NVA was certainly unconcerned about the future of women thrown out of the brothels even if it increased their physical vulnerability. Prostitutes who left the brothels and lodgings had little alternative but to work on streets which were less safe or else give up their trade and perhaps enter a reformatory.

The Birmingham and Midland branch of the NVA was also concerned about child abuse. Child abuse generated moral outrage. Radical feminist historians have suggested that the prosecution of, and campaigns against, child sexual abuse broke the conspiracy of silence around this issue and protected young women from aggressive male behaviour. Unfortunately the prosecutions of child abusers were not as effective as radical feminists suggest. To a large extent the NVA wielded a double-edged moral sword in the fight against sexual impurity. On the one hand, it sought to defend young girls from sexual abuse and espoused a sexual politics based upon protection. It prosecuted child abusers. On the other hand the abused girls were also punished as they were sent away from their families to a Home to be rehabilitated. However, social purity workers were successful in changing the law regarding child abuse. Eventually, after considerable campaigning, the Punishment of Incest Act was passed in 1908, which instituted a punishment for incest in civil law by stating that 'any male person who has carnal knowledge of a female person known to be his grand daughter, daughter, sister or mother is guilty of a misdemenour and liable to penal servitude of not less than 3 years, and not more than 7 years'. For the first time, male biological relatives could be put on trial for child abuse.

The NVA operated at what is sometimes perceived as a transitional moment in British politics when liberal individualism was being replaced by a more collectivist culture. The NVA was willing to use the emerging interventionist and middle-class State to regulate the private behaviour of its citizens. It viewed the criminal law as an agency of protection as well as repression and saw the State as an agency of change in that governments could - as in the Poor Law of 1834 - legislate to alter the moral behaviour of its citizens. Certainly the activities of the NVA reflected this new interventionist spirit because it used the regulatory powers of the State to institute proceedings against those who offended their particular middle-class moral code.

Various attempts were made by successive governments, individuals and reforming groups to eliminate prostitution or else to make it safe. In many ways, these attempts reflected the political climate of the period. At first, reformers tackled the problem of prostitution on a piecemeal basis by attempting to punish and reform the individual prostitute. With the growth of feminism a newer sympathetic approach was advocated which tackled the problem of prostitution at source. As the idea of *laissez faire* declined in popularity so the State intervened by attempting to make prostitution safe for the armed forces. By the end of the century the collectivist spirit was in the ascendant so new groups tried to cure the problem by changing the structure of society rather than attempting to plaster over the moral cracks.

Making Notes on *'Prostitution and its Repression'*

There is only a limited analysis of the historiography and quite a lot of narrative in this chapter because in 1995 when this book was written it was very much a new area of research. Use the headings of the sections to help you take notes. Also use the following questions to guide you as they are the type of questions which examiners may well pose in future.

1   What were the main causes of prostitution, according to historians, in the nineteenth century?
2   To what extent did penitentiaries aim to instil middle-class values into working-class inmates?
3   Why were the CDAs passed and why were they repealed? (or another way - how far was Butler responsible for the repeal of the CDAs?)
4   To what extent were the aims of the Ladies' Associations humanitarian?
5   How repressive was the NVA?

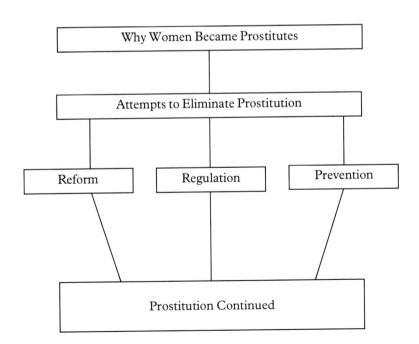

Summary - Prostitution and its Repression

Source-based questions on 'Prostitution and its Repression'

1 Portrait of Sien

Study the portrait on page 79, called *Sorrow*, which was drawn by Vincent Van Gogh. Although it is a European portrait, with sometimes quite different cultural and historical implications, it is an interesting piece of evidence to analyse. To fully understand even a simple drawing, it is perhaps important to know a little of its historical background. Sien, the object of this study by Van Gogh, was born in 1850. She was the eldest of ten children born to a Dutch working-class family who often sent her to an orphanage because they could not afford to keep her at home. By 1882 she had given birth to three children and had been treated for venereal disease at Lieden. Sien supplemented her income as a seamstress with prostitution until she became a model for Van Gogh who fell in love with her and proposed marriage. She refused and returned to prostitution. Much of the symbolism in the portrait reflects Van Gogh's as well as nineteenth-century attitudes towards penitent prostitutes (and indeed towards Sien) so you need to be aware of the personal as well as the historical context for this drawing.

Van Gogh wrote in a letter to his brother in 1881:

> I met a pregnant woman, deserted by the man whose child she carried. A pregnant woman who had to walk the streets in winter, had to earn her bread, you understand how.
>
> I took this woman for a model, and have worked with her all winter, I could not pay her full wages of a model, but that did not prevent my paying her rent, and thank God, so far I have been able to protect her and her child from hunger and cold by sharing my own bread with her. When I met this woman she attracted my attention because she looked ill. I made her take baths and as much nourishing food as I could afford, and she has become stronger. I went with her to Leyden, to the maternity hospital where she will be confined.

Look carefully at the portrait of Sien on page 79 and read the extract above.

a)   What do you think lilies of the valley and the spring blossom might indicate? (2 marks)

b)   Why do you think Van Gogh has drawn Sien in such a posture? (2 marks)
    Either

c)   In what way does the written source and your knowledge of the nineteenth century help you understand the portrait? (6 marks)
    Or

c)   What is the historical significance of this portrait? (6 marks)

CHAPTER 6

Women in Political Change

The slogan 'Votes for Women' embodies the popular image of women's political activity but women's role was extraordinarily more complex and diverse than participation in the campaigns for the franchise. Women from all social classes engaged in politics at a local and national level but the ways in which they participated were distinct from those of men. Because women were denied the vote they often played an indirect role in parliamentary affairs. Whatever their class background, most women acted in a supportive capacity, helping the men in their families to gain and retain power. Aristocratic women, Chartist women, and women members of political parties all shared a common goal of electing men who shared their political perspective. Outside Parliament and local electoral politics there were few legal restrictions prohibiting female participation in politics so pressure groups such as the Anti-Corn Law League, the Anti-Slavery Campaign, and the spontaneous politics involving riots and demonstrations drew large numbers of women.

Local issues, town improvements, educational development and social welfare reform were considered appropriate areas of political work because they were an extension of women's domestic role. The experience gained in such a wide range of political action encouraged some women to fight for their own rights. This eventually culminated in the campaigns for female suffrage which became the major issue for activists in the early part of the twentieth century.

1 National Politics

Without formal political power, women from the political classes affected events indirectly through their family connections. In addition, Whig ladies-in-waiting to the Queen wielded considerable influence in the close-knit political world of early Victorian England while political hostesses played a significant part in promoting politicians and political alignments within their aristocratic circles. Many a political career was advanced by timely wifely intervention. For example, the wives of both Palmerston and Disraeli entertained sympathisers on an impressive scale in order to consolidate political allegiances. Some women organised electoral campaigns and advised their husbands on political matters. The wives of many a nineteenth- and early twentieth-century Prime Minister acted as a confidante to whom was entrusted all the political secrets of the day, while other wives provided much-needed emotional support. For instance, Disraeli frequently consulted his wife and praised her fidelity because 'she believed in me when men despised me'. Nevertheless, political wives were expected to listen to, rather than advise, their husbands as Beatrice Potter, (later Beatrice Webb) whose relationship with Joseph Chamberlain ended because of her independent views, demonstrated:

1 I shall be absorbed into the life of a man, whose aims are not my
 aims; who will refuse me all freedom of thought in my intercourse
 with him; to whose career I shall have to subordinate all my life,
 mental and physical. ... The outward circumstances of the life of a
5 politician's wife would be distasteful to me, or rather they would be
 supremely demoralising. ... Once married I should of course
 subordinate my views to my husband's..

Upper-middle-class women exerted their own power through
patronage, for example by renting land or giving custom to those who
voted for their favoured candidate in the open hustings. Some women
exercised their political influence by pressurising their tenants to vote
according to their wishes: pledges to vote were often extracted from
prospective tenants before they were granted land. After 1832 women's
political influence of this type increased as newly enfranchised urban
shopkeepers were encouraged to vote for their customers' choice of
candidate. Historians have suggested that by such methods women were
reasonably successful in ensuring their views were indirectly represented
until the secret ballot of 1872.

Wealthy women were effective in politics because the men in their
families had political leverage in Parliament. At the beginning of the
century the majority of men did not have the vote and so had no
parliamentary influence to wield. As a result, women helped their
brothers, husbands and fathers to gain the franchise rather than to fight
battles of their own. Thus, during this period, women engaged in
political activity almost entirely for the benefit of others. In the early
campaigns to extend the male franchise, women were present in large
numbers. From 1819 onwards Female Reform Societies were founded
in many northern towns to help men gain the vote. At Peterloo in 1819,
Mary Fildes, President of the Female Reform Society of Manchester
shared the carriage of a leading speaker. In 1830-1, when the Whigs
were attempting to implement a measure of parliamentary reform,
female societies were formed to support male suffrage and their
members rioted alongside men in towns across the country during the
reading of each Bill.

a) Chartism 1838-58

Chartism, a popular radical movement which campaigned for universal
male suffrage, attracted large numbers of women. It has been estimated
that there were at least 80 Female Chartist Associations in Britain. The
numbers involved in each local group differed but, not surprisingly,
some of the strong Chartist areas of Birmingham, Nottingham and
Yorkshire attracted the largest support. For example, leaders claimed as

many as 17,000 female members in Birmingham.

Like most women involved in parliamentary politics, Chartist women joined these associations in order to support the men in their families. Most women who joined Female Chartist Associations were married women between the ages of 20 and 40 who had either been involved in other forms of working-class radical protest or whose husbands were engaged in Chartist activity. Many wives took an active role in furthering the Chartist movement. Indeed, few male Chartist leaders could have continued without the support of their wives who gave invaluable assistance to the Chartist campaigns. For example, Lucy Vincent helped her husband Henry publish the Western Vindicator, a popular Chartist newspaper, from their home in Bath and many wives willingly worked to provide an income for their family whilst their husbands were imprisoned for Chartist activities. Only rarely did such women demand universal suffrage (votes for all women as well as for all men over 21) because the male working-class vote was seen as a political priority in that it was hoped that it would ensure higher pay, improved working conditions and a higher standard of living, all of which would benefit the whole family. Class affiliations therefore took precedence over female concerns with many Chartist women believing that the male vote was a step forward for working-class people. Women thought that when the male working-class franchise was secured it would be easier for themselves to gain the vote. Rather than ally themselves with middle-class feminists, female Chartists campaigned for universal male suffrage because they considered it inappropriate to grant the vote to the propertied female at the expense of the unrepresented male worker, which is what middle-class female activists wanted.

Many male Chartist leaders were sympathetic to female suffrage but thought it politically expedient to postpone doing anything about it. Apparently William Lovett, one of the early founders of Chartism, wished to include women's suffrage in the charter but had been overruled by other leaders who argued that it would delay male suffrage. Chartist men sometimes initiated women's participation in the Chartist movement, formed women's organisations and encouraged women to speak at meetings. As a result, women's associations were often male dominated with men speaking at female clubs and serving on their committees. In Hebden Bridge all the committee members of the female Chartist society were male. However, each local group organised independently so rules and regulations varied tremendously. Some Women's Chartist Associations excluded men except when invited. Women in other associations often met separately from men, heard their own guest speakers, voted for their own committee and passed their own resolutions.

Because women acted in a supportive capacity, and because they were defined by their role in the family, their activities were significantly different from those of men. Women were encouraged to join the large demonstrations and meetings, dressed in the white and green Chartist colours, in the hope that their presence would lend respectability to the proceedings. As a general rule women were much more involved in the social events than the political side of the movement. They sewed the banners and flags; they organised balls, dances and tea parties, for which they prepared food, put up displays, decorated halls and arranged speakers; they taught in Chartist chapels and Sunday schools; they raised funds by door-to-door collections and sold knitted handkerchiefs, books and other items; they acted as newsagents for the Chartist newspapers; they encouraged women to buy goods from sympathetic shopkeepers to boycott those who were antagonistic to the Chartist cause.

Women did not always conform to the feminine stereotype. Occasionally women were involved in picketing and violent activity as were the Lancashire women who volunteered to provide themselves with arms and fight alongside the men and the women of the Nottingham branch who proclaimed that 'tis better to die by the sword than by famine'. At large gatherings capable female speakers were said to entrance their audiences when arguing for the need for a male working-class franchise. Many Chartist women thus gained political experience in public speaking at a time when few middle-class women had the opportunity to do so. A few wrote long, influential newspaper articles proclaiming the need for democracy, for class struggle, and education for women. They also composed songs and wrote poems (the famous Chartist poem, 'The Lion of Freedom' is attributed to a Welsh woman).

By the mid 1840s the number of women involved in Chartism was thought to have decreased. It used to be argued that as the Chartist movement became better organised and more highly structured women became marginalised within working-class politics because they felt ill at ease in the hierarchical committees and delegations to an all-male Parliament which this entailed. However, this interpretation has been revised in recent years. After 1847 there was supposedly a revival in female Chartism and there were reports of large female attendances at Chartist rallies. Similarly, with the decline of Chartism generally, women's participation in parliamentary politics was said to have decreased and when the franchise question was raised again in the 1860s the role of women was thought to be negligible but, once again, new research indicates that women were involved in the campaigns surrounding the 1867 Reform Act. For instance, 1,499 women signed the 1866 suffrage petition and many women were involved in the networks of organisation around this.

b) The Growth of Political Parties

Before the introduction of the secret ballot of 1872, voting was a public affair whereby candidates were often elected by a show of hands. Under this system powerful landowners and other wealthy men were able to exert undue influence over the voters by buying drinks, promising jobs or other similar enticements. As more and more men were enfranchised and voting became a private concern, an efficient party organisation was essential. Both major parties therefore set up organisations to attract the mass electorate and women played a significant part in electoral campaigns. In 1884 women were admitted to the newly created Primrose League, the Tory Party electoral association, as Dames or associates. The Ladies' Grand Council, the female executive wing, was dominated by titled ladies but despite its status and the high public profile of a few talented leaders, it merely rubber stamped Conservative Party policies. Conservative women wielded greater influence in local groups, called Habitations, which were more democratic and representative of a larger cross-section of the population. In some Habitations women held executive positions. Grantham in Lincolnshire had a women-only Habitation which was also one of the most powerful. Here, and in other areas, women acted as unpaid canvassers, distributed leaflets, and occasionally spoke at public meetings in support of the male candidate. Debutantes, used to being cossetted and chaperoned, were sometimes found canvassing in shabby and squalid areas in support of family members. As one feminist historian has noted, physical labour was unusual for this class of women who were used to employing an army of domestic servants to perform menial work. Nevertheless, members willingly - or otherwise - undertook tasks such as those outlined below:

1 They assembled and addressed 13,000 envelopes, folded 13,000
   addresses, addressed another 13,000 envelopes, wrote out 13,000
   polling cards, and put them in the second batch of envelopes.
   Everything was checked, the outvoters were readdressed, and all
5 this was done inside a week ... willingly done without fee or reward
   or even a cup of tea.

Women, quite naturally, also organised fetes, afternoon teas and soirees because this was seen as an extension of their charity work and therefore more appropriate than other types of public activity. Indeed, the women of the Primrose League publicly stated that they did not wish to govern the country. On the contrary, Conservative women wished to help men get elected to Government which in turn would lead the country to peace and prosperity.

Similarly, Liberal women organised party work but they were less deferential to their men. The Women's Liberal Federation, founded in 1886, was affiliated to the Liberal Federation but was an autonomous, women-only organisation which offered invaluable political training by encouraging women to participate in local and national politics.

Delegates at Annual Meetings claimed the right to define party policy and aimed to preserve women's separate political voice within the party. Dominated by Nonconformist, feminist sympathisers, the Federation supported suffrage and radical social policies concerning health, housing, education, temperance and social purity (see page 93). They were particularly influential in the selection of potential candidates and campaigned only for those who agreed with their policies on suffrage and moral reform. To some extent they were successful: a number of opponents of women's suffrage were defeated in the 1880 election as a result of Federation intervention.

In the early days of the Independent Labour Party, founded in 1893, women were viewed as co-leaders even though their role was less visible than men's. Women spoke at public meetings, wrote articles in newspapers and journals and helped develop party policy. Some tasks were still viewed as specifically female, so women, not men, organised the picnics, concerts and Socialist Sunday schools. In 1906 the Women's Labour League was formed from the embryonic Labour Party to increase women's political involvement in public bodies and to campaign for social reform. Like their Tory and Liberal counterparts these women took a less prominent role than their male comrades within party politics, campaigning for electoral success when they themselves were without the vote.

c) Pressure-group Politics

Banned from parliamentary politics, many middle-class women participated in pressure-group politics where their organisational flair was welcomed. From 1841, women's skills were utilised by the Anti-Corn Law League to run bazaars and fairs, to collect subscriptions and to organise petitions. Richer women created 40-shilling freeholds (the amount of land needed to qualify a man for the electorate in county constituencies) from their large property holdings which were used to obtain votes for supporters of the League. In particular women's support was welcomed in pressure-group politics which had a philanthropic or moral dimension because it confirmed the sentiment that women were the carers and guardians of righteousness. Quaker and evangelical women dominated the groups which aimed to abolish slavery in the British colonies. In 1828 the Birmingham Female Society for the Relief of British Negro Slaves, one of the most important organisations of the anti-slavery movement, was formed. Two years later female anti-slavery societies were founded in many other towns and cities. These led to the boycott of slave-grown sugar and other goods, made considerable financial contributions, sold home-produced goods to raise money, distributed thousands of leaflets and did valuable propaganda work. Unlike American women, anti-slavery campaigners in Britain rarely spoke to large audiences, preferring to work in smaller, intimate gatherings, but their considerable involvement contributed to the success of the campaign. Similarly women tried to ban the sale and drinking of alcohol by joining the temperance movement which emerged at the same time. Historians have suggested that temperance was of particular interest to women because drink was associated with the demise of family values and frequently led to wife battering and poverty. In an attempt to stop this perceived moral decline women visited schools to found branches of the Band of Hope, the children's wing of the temperance movement, and encouraged people to sign the abstinence pledge.

Ad hoc and spontaneous politics, in which groups were formed for a specific purpose, drew women in large numbers. This type of direct action suited women, most of whom were unable to spare the time (or else were discouraged from doing so) to sit at meetings for hours on end discussing organisational policy. Thus some of the demonstrations, disturbances and riots which characterised the first half of the nineteenth century were inspired and led by women. Much of women's participation in *ad hoc* politics was based on concerns about family values. For example, in 1820 when George IV banished his wife, Queen Caroline, from the court, refused her access to her daughter, and tried to divorce her on the grounds of her much-publicised adultery, many women organised petitions and led demonstrations against his conduct. Violent protests often arose because women were unable to provide for their families. Women, alongside men, smashed James Hargreaves' spinning jenny, destroyed one of Arkwright's factories and attacked weaving looms invented by Edmund Cartwright because they feared that these new inventions would increase unemployment. Women also participated in the Poor Law and Rebecca Riots of 1839 and 1842 which protested against the Bastilles, the name they gave the newly built workhouses. In the Plug Riots of 1842 women helped remove the plugs from steam-engine boilers in textile factories as a protest against the rejection of the second Chartist petition. In the food riots which took place in the early part of the nineteenth century against high prices, low wages, and food shortages, middle-aged women and mothers with young children often played a leading role. One Manchester woman was hanged in 1812 for stealing provisions from carts entering the town. Over 40 years later, women were still engaging in similar action: 200 women and children stole bread and cakes from the windows they had smashed in Crediton, Devon.

2 Local Politics

Local politics were often considered to be women's realm as they were seen as an extension of the home, charity and philanthropic work. Women engaged in local politics in towns and cities which had a history of women's participation, or else which had a large population of middle-class women with time, money and energy to spare. For the most part these women were Nonconformists (by religion), Liberal (in politics) and supported women's suffrage. Not surprisingly they took a radical stance on many issues of social welfare.

In 1869 single or widowed ratepaying women were given the right to vote for municipal councils and the later county councils. By the 1880s women formed between 12 and 25 per cent of the local electorate, even though they were debarred from becoming councillors. In fact, unsuccessful attempts were made to thwart the legal system in order to get elected. In London three women served as councillors until they were unseated by the courts on technical grounds. In 1894 women were allowed to participate in parish, district and vestry (church) councils. When in 1907 women were admitted to all aspects of local government only a few were eligible, because of property qualifications, for election. Even so, this small number of women was said to have carried out a prodigious amount of work. They helped to provide amenities such as public lavatories, baths and parks and, after 1902, persuaded Local Education Authorities to provide school meals. Committed to improving the towns in which they lived, they paved, drained and sanitised their local areas, demolished or repaired slum property, built decent housing stock and created garden suburbs. Their endeavours, combined with public health reform, contributed to the reduction in infant mortality and allegedly helped to make towns and cities pleasanter places in which to live. However, it was sometimes difficult to persuade women to become involved in council work as the following quote from a woman political activist writing in 1897 shows:

1 That many more women did not from the first take up this work, is, I think, greatly attributable to their having failed to recognise that, although their duties upon these governing bodies might never bring them into personal touch with those whom they desired to 5 serve, in the same way as a member of a School Board may be in touch with the scholars whose interests she has at heart, and a Guardian with the inmates of a workhouse, yet the work affects human needs in a very special manner. It is a pity that we have not more faith, that we need to see in order to believe.
10 It is very difficult to realise that even so dull a matter as street-cleansing has its effect on the health and well-being of the community, whilst the efficient lighting of the slums of our cities has a purifying and beneficial influence upon the crowded life in our courts and alleys? What more congenial occupation could 15 there be than the provision of open spaces for the children to play in? What more useful one than the supervision of the Baths and washhouses? What more elevating one than the administration of Public Libraries? All these things minister to the needs of the dwellers in our one and two-roomed tenements.

20 But the work par excellence for women is that of the Health Committee. ... We deal with indifferent and bad landlords ... force them to give to their tenants such sanitary conditions, as without our aid they could not secure for themselves.

From 1834 women were eligible to vote for Poor Law Guardians but it was not until 1875 that the first woman was elected to this position. Like the local franchise, these rights did not apply to married women until 1894 when the property qualification was also abolished thus increasing the number of women Poor Law Guardians considerably. By 1900, 1,000 women were Poor Law Guardians. Poor Law work did not attract large numbers of women because it was considered less congenial than education or local council work. Visiting the unwashed poor, the chronically sick, the venereally diseased and the aged infirm in workhouses was a thankless task which only the most devoted and determined would consider, as this quote from Patricia Hollis' *Ladies Elect*, published in 1987, confirms:

1 Women nosed around those sanitary facilities and parts of the hospitals and workhouses which the gentlemen very rarely visit said Miss Thorburn of Liverpool. Mrs Evans suspected that the ophthalmia and ringworm she noted spread because 56 girls
5 bathed in one tub of water, and shared half a dozen towels, five dirty brushes and two and a half combs between them. Another workhouse, they found, had two small hand basins for 120 women, and WCs without paper, which were locked at night. Some infirmaries had no lavatories at all, and the sick had go downstairs
10 and outdoors to 'a sort of a shed' on winter nights. Rural unions were even more backward. Dunmow in 1904 swarmed with rats, Billericay in the 1890s had no lavatories at all.

Women often faced hostility from male Guardians who not only resented women *per se* but resented their criticism of the sanitation, the food, the clothing, the sleeping arrangements and the treatment of inmates within the workhouses. But, despite an uphill struggle, the work of the female Guardians mitigated the worst excesses of workhouse life as the care of children in the workhouse grew better, sanitation improved and the sick and the elderly were given greater respect. In addition, women Guardians were said to improve Poor Law administration by making it more efficient.

When the 1870 Education Act was passed women were eligible to vote for and to serve on the newly created School Boards. Women's participation on School Boards was considered highly appropriate for it was seen as an extension of the home and the family. School Boards were responsible for the education of children from the age of five and often undertook the training of girl pupil-teachers. These Boards, consisting of between nine and fifteen members, were generally run on party lines. School Boards gave women the opportunity to develop their organisational skills: some influential feminists became powerful figures on their local School Board and used them to initiate educational change. Most women involved in School Boards took their role extremely seriously as this extract from a female Board member in 1901 attests:

1 A thoroughly equipped manager should know of Kindergarten and Infant Teaching; of the work of the first two Standards; of house-wifery, theoretical and practical; of physical exercises; of voice production and of drawing. Not, I mean, that she need be
5 competent to teach all these things, but she should know the principles which underlie these various branches of elementary teaching ...
Be not too ready to speak at the Board and managers' meetings; loyally abide by the vote of the majority; never be the partisan of a
10 particular teacher. ... A really effective member must have mother wit and contrive to introduce things so that the authorities may see their value ...
Teachers have a solitary life, although they live in a crowd ... are very open to the help that a sympathetic manager can offer. Begin
15 by encouraging, and not by being critical. Classes are of necessity very large, and the time and attention given to seemingly insignificant details of behaviour are the result of long experience.

Some female members of School Boards campaigned for radical policies within schools, argued against corporal punishment, advocated cookery lessons for boys as well as girls, tried to widen the curriculum to include PE, music and nature study, and criticised payment by results. One leading suffragist, Lydia Becker, 'did not know why cooking was considered an exclusive subject for girls. If she had her own way every boy in Manchester would be taught to mend his own socks and cook his own chops. When School Boards were abolished in 1902 women's role was threatened because they were not allowed to be elected on to the town and county councils which took over responsibility for education.

What characterised the women who worked in local government was their dedication and commitment. For the most part women were more assiduous than their male colleagues, set higher standards and took on the role of virtually full-time, unpaid workers in their chosen fields. It was believed that local politics would enable women to enter national politics as they were becoming an increasingly influential, experienced electorate as well as gaining valuable political experience by holding local office. Many of them therefore wanted a vote of their own in parliamentary elections.

3 Towards the Vote

On a sunny June day in 1913, Emily Wilding Davidson, prompted by a desire to gain publicity for women's suffrage, went to the Derby, rushed out on to the racecourse, grabbed the reins of the King's horse and tried to stop the race. She was unsuccessful, died of head injuries a few days later and was mourned as the first suffragette martyr. This spectacular event has dominated the popular image of the suffrage movement but is really only a relatively minor episode in its history. The important questions raised by historians about the campaigns for votes for women centre around a) the reasons why women wanted the vote, b) the composition of the franchise movement, c) the issue of militancy, and d) an assessment of the movement's success.

a) Why Women Wanted the Vote

Women wanted to participate in the democratic process in the same way as men for a number of different reasons. Two-thirds of adult males had gained the vote in the Reform Acts of 1832, 1867 and 1884, but all women, like criminals and patients in lunatic asylums, were denied what was perceived as a basic human right in a democratic country. Many people considered it inappropriate to claim that Britain had a representative government when more than half of the population was disenfranchised on the grounds of gender. It was perceived as particularly inequitable because voting rights throughout the nineteenth century were based on property qualifications. Although women owned and managed properties and paid rates and taxes, they were not represented in Parliament. In 1884, for example, 30,000 women tenants saw their male labourers enfranchised while they remained excluded.

Voting had a symbolic significance for women who believed that its absence reflected their second-class status. The franchise was seen as a symbol of citizenship from which women were excluded. The vote also had a practical significance for it was seen as a means to the end of greater social justice. Governments could and did easily ignore the problems and the concerns of the unrepresented. Throughout the nineteenth century there was an increased importance attached to the power of the electorate. As more and more men were enfranchised, so laws were enacted which reflected the wishes of the voters. For instance, after 1832 the Whigs passed a series of laws such as the Poor Law Amendment Act and the Factory Acts which represented the particular interests of the newly enfranchised middle class. When many working-class men received the vote in 1867 educational reform and improved trade union legislation reflected their new political status. Many women believed that their own particular needs would be met by Parliament if they acquired the vote. Women often earned less than half a male wage, were denied educational opportunities, and were barred from certain employment. Sweated labour existed throughout the country as working-class women continued to be exploited. It was believed that the granting of the right to vote to women would lead to an improvement in the pay, conditions and life of working-class women. Furthermore, as moral guardians of the race, it was believed that they would persuade Parliament to legislate against the sexual immorality of many men. Finally the vote would be a culmination of the economic, educational and legal gains of women.

As a result, women campaigned for female suffrage. Although the issue of women's suffrage was raised in the 1830s, it was not until the skilled male worker gained the vote in 1867 and women were excluded once again that a movement as such emerged. From then on different groups of women struggled to put the 'votes for women' issue on the political agenda.

b) Was it a Middle-class Movement?

At first glance it seems as if the suffrage movement was dominated by middle-class women who wanted the vote on the same terms as middle-class men. All too often the suffrage movement has been condemned for having a middle-class and elitist perspective. Indeed, the suffrage movement has been associated with a minority group of privileged women who sought to extend their rights at the expense of the less fortunate. It has been argued that middle-class women, frustrated at their restricted lives, led the National Union of Women's Suffrage Societies to seek the vote for women 'as it is and may be given to men' which in essence meant a property vote for middle-class women. Women wanted suffrage on the same terms as male electors - householders in boroughs and in the counties, owners of freeholds and the renters of land and houses above a certain value. Initially it was an elite call for equality. In 1832 only a few rich women would have qualified for the vote but as each new Reform Act enfranchised different groups of men so more and more women would have become eligible under the property qualifications. Contemporaries of the suffragists as well as historians have criticised their uncritical acceptance of property qualifications. It was argued that these privileged women did not identify with less fortunate working-class women. However the male franchise was given only in tranches, step by slow step, which is how many women perceived their own campaign. Furthermore, very few have criticised the male suffrage movements of the 1830s and the 1860s when they demanded a restrictive vote.

Research also suggests that in the early years of the suffrage movement the campaign was dominated by middle-class women. Lydia Becker who founded the Manchester Women's Suffrage Committee was one such woman. When all the small local organisations joined together

THE COMMON CAUSE, AUGUST 17, 1911.

IF YOU LIKE THIS PAPER, FILL IN THE ORDER FORM ON THE BACK PAGE AND HAND IT TO YOUR NEWSAGENT.

The Common Cause,

The Organ of the National Union of

Women's Suffrage

Societies.

VOL. III.   No. 123.   Registered as a Newspaper.   AUGUST 17, 1911.   ONE PENNY.

TAXATION AND REPRESENTATION.

Pit Brow Girl: Ah doan't see why ah should pay to keep thee, lad!   What good has tha bin to me?

Representative of the "People": But my good woman didn't I vote last week to deprive 6,000 of you of your livelihood, in order that you shouldn't black your pretty faces with coal dust?

Pit Brow Girl: 'Twould be fairer then, so 'twould, for thee to keep uz, and not uz keep thee!

NUWSS propaganda

to form the National Union of Women's Suffrage Societies (the NUWSS) in 1897 it was comprised, at least at leadership level, of women from notable families. These were exceptional political activists, many of whom had been involved in other middle-class campaigns such as education, employment and property rights. The campaign for the vote was a continuation of these struggles.

Until fairly recently it was commonly assumed that working-class women did not participate in the suffrage movement. This may have been the case in the early years but by the last decade of the century the movement ceased to be completely full of the middle class. In the 1890s, as Liddington and Norris have shown, radical suffragists worked hard to involve working-class women in the campaign, particularly in the major cotton towns of Lancashire and Cheshire, and they encouraged hundreds of female cotton workers to join the movement. Dinner-hour meetings were held at the mill gates and evening meetings were held on street corners and in town squares. In 1903 the Lancashire and Cheshire Women Textile and Other Workers Representation Committee (LCWT) was founded which was the first organisation of working women for the vote. As a result of the activities of these suffragists ten local suffrage committees were established in the major cotton towns. Cotton workers received better wages than most working-class women, were perceived to be more independent, were unionised and were relatively easily organised outside the factory gates. Reasons such as these account for the popularity of the suffrage movement amongst working-class women in the north and its lack of support elsewhere. Outside of the northern cotton towns the Co-operative Women's Guild campaigned for the vote but the success rate in attracting support was not as high as it was in the cotton towns.

In 1903 a new organisation, the Women's Social and Political Union (WSPU) was formed by Emmeline Pankhurst and her daughters Christabel and Sylvia. A few historians have condemned the elitism of the WSPU because it recruited rich, influential women rather than working-class women. One of the first historians to research the Pankhursts viewed them as sex-starved maniacs with lesbian tendencies who led a half-crazed bunch of upper-class masculinised women. This caricature trivialises the crucial impact of the WSPU on the suffrage and the labour movements. Initially the WSPU was active in socialist as well as suffrage politics, working alongside the Independent Labour Party (ILP). Between 1903 and 1906 the WSPU did valuable propaganda work in the cotton towns, helped by Annie Kenney, who was to become Christabel Pankhurst's right-hand woman, and her sisters - all mill workers - and Hannah Mitchell a dressmaker's apprentice from Bolton who later became famous for her writings on working-class life. This emphasis on working-class recruitment is thought to have been lost when the WSPU moved to London in 1906. Yet the WSPU had its working-class branches. Until at least 1908 the WSPU was active in

Woolwich, Lewisham and Greenwich and organised meetings and demonstrations outside the Woolwich Arsenal, a huge armaments factory. In 1912 Sylvia Pankhurst trained speakers, organised meetings and led several working-class deputations to the House of Commons.

Furthermore, most of the suffrage organisations supported working-class women's issues. When women who worked on the pit-brow, sorting coal, campaigned against protective legislation (see pages 58 to 61) in 1911 they drew support from all the suffrage groups. *Votes for Women*, the WSPU newspaper, carried main features and articles about the deputations and meetings of the pit-brow workers and sent Annie Kenney, an indomitable woman and charismatic speaker, to Wigan to organise public meetings. Similar support was given to the chain makers and barmaids when their livelihoods were threatened. Armed with the franchise, suffragists believed that they would be able to give still greater protection to working-class women.

To dismiss the suffrage movement as middle class is therefore too simple. Firstly both middle-class and working-class women campaigned for the vote, albeit in various numbers. Secondly, even a limited female franchise was only ever seen as a means to the end of greater social justice for all. Finally, the militant action, particularly of the suffragettes did not conform to the behaviour expected of middle-class women.

c) Differences between the Organisations: the Question of Militancy

Historians tend to see the suffrage movement as made up of a number of separate groups all campaigning for the vote rather than as one political movement. Indeed, it is customary to stress the differences rather than the similarities between the groups. Firstly, it is argued that the structure of each organisation differed: that the WSPU was run by the despotic Pankhurst family, aided by a few loyal and unquestioning lieutenants, who dictated their wishes to an acquiescent membership, whereas the NUWSS and the Women's Freedom League (WFL) were considered to be democratic and sensitive to the needs of the women who joined their groups. Secondly, it is claimed that the membership of the two organisations varied: that both the NUWSS and the WFL accepted sympathetic men, whereas the WSPU remained a separatist, female society. It is pointed out that by 1912 the WSPU was stridently anti-male, advocating chastity for men as well as votes for women. Thirdly, it is maintained that the aims of the organisations were distinctive: that whereas the WSPU increasingly saw the vote as an end in itself, the other groups saw it as a means by which to improve the position of women. Finally it is argued that the methods used by these groups were significantly dissimilar as the suffragists were deemed to be law abiding whereas the suffragettes constantly broke the law.

However, this analysis is misleading. Although it is true that, like most campaigns for political equality, the suffrage movement was divided into several strands which followed differing policies on organisation and tactics, the more significant fact is that they shared much in common. Large numbers of women joined both a militant and a non-militant organisation, paid two membership fees, attended different sets of meetings and campaigned for both groups. Such women certainly did not see the suffrage movement as made up of antagonistic groups vying for members. Much of the debate about the differences between the two main organisations (the WSPU and the NUWSS) centres around the issue of militancy. It has been commonly assumed that there was a division between the militants (the WSPU), called the suffragettes, and the constitutionalists (the NUWSS), known as the suffragists. However, this is not a very helpful distinction because militancy is an elastic concept which changed its meaning between 1860 and 1914.

Historians have held differing views on what militancy was and when it began. It has generally been associated with the activities of the suffragettes - such as smashing windows and setting fire to buildings. However, militancy had a different meaning in the early nineteenth century than it was to have in the early twentieth. Harriet Taylor was considered militant when she voiced her opinions to J.S. Mill and published with him a book on the rights of women. When Lydia Becker tried to influence the government through its own back benchers, petitioned Parliament, wrote letters to the press, published articles in periodicals and spoke in public, she challenged accepted norms of female behaviour and she too was thought to be militant. Many of the early actions of suffrage workers had become stale by the end of the nineteenth century. Whereas it was considered daring for women to speak in public in the early part of the century, by the 1890s most of the population was more accustomed to it and was inclined to treat it as nothing out of the ordinary.

When the WSPU erupted on to the political scene in 1903 the word militant took on a new meaning. As Emmeline Pankhurst noted, the WSPU distinguished itself from the other suffrage groups by the use of the word militant. It was a word often associated with violent tactics but even in the short time between 1903 and 1914 what was considered to be militancy altered. Militancy is said to have begun in 1905 when a Cabinet Minister, speaking in the Manchester Free Trade Hall, was interrupted by Christabel Pankhurst and Annie Kenney who called out 'Votes for women'. They were arrested, put on trial, and eventually sent to prison. Heckling at Cabinet Ministers' meetings became a popular suffragette activity. Women hid in church organs all night or entered meetings with a respectable man in tow as camouflage in order to shout out 'Votes for women' when the meeting began. Women sitting in the public gallery interrupted important speeches made by MPs in the

House of Commons and pestered Liberal politicians to such an extent that women were banned from their political meetings unless they had been vetted.

Nevertheless, this was a period of 'mild militancy' - of deputations, marches, demonstrations, meetings, heckling and bye-election work. The second phase of militancy can be said to have begun with a stone through the Prime Minister's windows at 10 Downing Street in 1912. From this point militancy entered a much more dangerous phase. Attacks on property became more and more extensive and violent. In March 1912 the whole of London's West End suffered - women in relays smashed windows in Piccadilly and the Haymarket, and when they were arrested the next group struck Regent Street and the Strand, followed by Oxford Circus and Bond Street. A couple of days later when the police were expecting a demonstration in Parliament Square hundreds of women attacked Knightsbridge windows instead. During 1913 and 1914 suffragette violence escalated as private houses, churches and public places were bombed. Race courses and golf courses had slogans such as 'Votes or War', 'Justice before Sport', 'No votes, no Golf', cut and burned into their turf. Telephone wires were cut, greenhouses at Kew Gardens were destroyed and letters in post boxes were ruined by black fluid being poured on them. Railway stations, sports pavilions and empty houses were destroyed with bombs. In February 1913 Lloyd George's newly built Surrey house was badly damaged by a bomb planted by Emily Wilding Davidson. Mary Richardson, later called Slasher Mary, attacked the *Rokeby Venus,* a famous painting by Velasquez which hung in the National Gallery. Some historians have suggested that this militancy culminated in the death of Emily Davidson at the Derby but violence continued long after her death. Women who engaged in this type of militant action faced imprisonment and forcible feeding if and when they went on hunger strike - as they often did.

Only the more violent actions of the WSPU have been categorised by historians as militant. Militancy has generally been defined as violent acts against property. If this definition of militancy is widened to include direct action in the support of an ideal, then other groups can also be deemed militant. The rent strike of the East London Federation of Suffragettes (ELFS), the campaigns in the north by working-class women, and the Women's Tax Resistance League may, for example, also be included. Tax resistance was initiated by the WFL in 1908 and over 100 members were imprisoned for various offences. For these middle-class women, going to prison was considered extremely militant because of its association with debauched and unrepentant criminals. The WFL also arranged for some of its members to chain themselves to the grille in the House of Commons and initiated the boycott of the 1911 census. Clashes with the police, carried out by the ELFS, were often violent and physically dangerous, resulting in injuries and broken bones.

Thus when the question of militancy is discussed both the meaning of the word and the way it was used by contemporaries must be examined. What was considered shocking in the 1860s had ceased to be so by 1905, and heckling, which led to Christabel's Pankhurst's arrest in 1905, was so commonplace by 1910 that it was generally thought to be unworthy of press comment. By 1913 militancy meant violent action against property. If the war had not begun in 1914 militancy might have escalated still further to gain an even more violent meaning. Thus when we raise the question of militancy we must firstly put it into historical context.

Historians have sometimes argued that the militancy of the WSPU destroyed support for votes for women because it alienated sympathetic Liberal ministers. This is not so. Militancy may have been a convenient excuse to avoid giving the vote to women but it was not the real reason. The long peaceful campaign which was waged before 1905 had not persuaded the House of Commons to pass legislation. Even, in 1910, when the WSPU called off its militant actions and adopted peaceful campaign tactics women were not granted the vote.

d) How Successful was the Suffrage Movement?

If one applies the most commonly used criterion for assessing success, (the achievement of one's objectives), the suffrage movement quite obviously failed: women had not gained the vote by the time the movement ceased most of its activities with the outbreak of war in 1914. Even after more than 50 years of campaigning, no government was prepared to enfranchise women because the change that was sought lacked widespread male popular support. However, the concept of partial success has historical validity and it is worth exploring how far the suffrage movement brought closer the achievement of votes for women. Despite setbacks, by 1914 suffrage had certainly become the foremost political question for women and was firmly on the national agenda.

However, even though suffrage eventually became headline news, no political party was prepared to adopt women's suffrage as party policy. As a result, all suffrage bills in Parliament were private members' bills, which meant that they had little chance of success. No bill for women's suffrage ever got beyond its second reading. When the first amendment on women's suffrage was debated in 1867 there were 71 votes for and 123 against. Practically every year for the following 40 years a women's franchise bill was introduced and failed. Not only did these private members' bills fail but the debates that took place on them were either facetious or downright hostile. In 1905 MPs debated, with mock seriousness, a measure for hours - to compel carts on the road to carry rear lights - in order to avoid giving time to a bill on women's suffrage.

Women's suffrage was unsuccessful in gaining wholesale party support for a number of different reasons. It has been argued that the Conservatives disliked any extension of democracy, that the Liberals were convinced that women would vote Conservative, and that the Labour Party preferred universal franchise to a limited female vote. However, such an interpretation ignores disagreements within the parties concerned.

In the Conservative Party the leadership was sympathetic towards votes for women over a considerable period. For instance, Prime Ministers Disraeli, Lord Salisbury initially, Balfour, and Bonar Law all paid lip service to female suffrage. Women's suffrage resolutions were also passed at Annual Conferences even though the Primrose League held 'no opinion on the question'. It therefore appears that votes for women had some measure of success in winning support within the Conservative Party. However, there is no evidence of any great commitment by their leaders to implement women's suffrage whilst they held office. This was largely because of the antagonistic attitude of Conservative back benchers towards any extension of the franchise.

Whereas the Conservative leadership supported votes for women and the rank and file opposed it, the opposite was true of the Liberals. Suffragists were constantly unsuccessful in persuading the leadership of the Liberals to give women votes. Gladstone disliked the idea of Women's Suffrage and let it be known that he and any government he formed would resist any amendment to enfranchise women in the 1867 Reform Bill. Historians have also pinpointed the entrenched position of Asquith (Prime Minister 1908-16) in blocking any progress towards votes for women. Indeed, Asquith refused to support the 1910 Conciliation Bill which would have enfranchised about a million women with the result that it was consigned to a Committee and subsequently failed. Further Conciliation Bills in 1911 and 1912 which would have given some women the vote were equally unsuccessful. When the Franchise and Registration Bill, designed to stop plural voting, was debated, women's suffrage was to be included in an amendment but when the Speaker ruled that this amendment changed the nature of the Bill it was withdrawn. Similarly a private members' bill of 1913 was defeated by 47 votes. Nevertheless, the suffrage movement succeeded both in obtaining grass-roots Liberal support as well as eventually gaining approval from some leading figures such as Lloyd George.

The Labour Representation Committee, which became the Labour Party in 1906, gave an equally complex response. It saw universal suffrage as being of greater importance than what was perceived as an elitist measure to give the franchise to women householders. However, even within such a small party there was a variety of views on the issue. John Burns, a notable trade unionist was totally opposed to votes for women but Keir Hardie and George Lansbury were strong supporters. Local groups often supported women's suffrage: the Woolwich Labour Party for example worked with the WSPU. Members of the Woolwich

Labour Party consistently supported the aims and methods of the WSPU because they realised that even a limited extension of the franchise would still give the vote to working-class widows and spinsters who were householders. Eventually in 1912 the Labour Party became the first major political party to support votes for women. However, support for female suffrage from such a minority party (the Labour Party had only 42 MPs at the time) could not ensure success in parliament.

With a few notable exceptions, votes for women remained unpopular and therefore unsuccessful within the confines of the House of Commons. Parliament probably reflected the attitudes of the majority of men in the country. Few governments would risk passing such controversial measures as votes for women without popular support. Outside Parliament the suffrage movement was decidedly unsuccessful in persuading most of the nation to support female franchise. This is reflected in popular music hall songs, the banning of women from certain places, and the increasing level of violence in the crowds that gathered around women's demonstrations. Fear of militancy closed many of the country's art galleries and museums to the public completely or sometimes to women only. The rule of 'No muffs, wrist bags or sticks' was widespread: the Royal Academy and the Tate Gallery were closed to women and the British Museum announced that:

1 The British museum is open to men, and also to women if accompanied by men who are willing to vouch for their good behaviour and take full responsibility. Unaccompanied women are only allowed in on presentation of a letter of introduction from a
5 responsible person vouching for the bearer's good behaviour and accepting responsibility for her acts.

The occasions on which women had to put up with violent sexual harassment were numerous: they were often intimidated, harassed, and the victims of anti-suffrage rioting. Recent research indicates that many suffragettes were violently and indecently assaulted when they participated in demonstrations. Antagonistic men often sexually harassed women on demonstrations, ripping their clothes and whispering obscenities in their ear. Even Mrs Pankhurst had to be rescued by policemen from an angry crowd of men in Newton Abbot, Devon when she tried to speak, all of which signifies the lack of public approval for votes for women.

The suffrage movement was equally unsuccessful in persuading the majority of women to join the struggle for the vote. In the early part of the twentieth century there were approximately 10.5 million women in Britain and only a small percentage of them belonged to the suffrage movement. Some women even campaigned against votes for women. In 1889 a protest against Women's Suffrage was signed by a number of well-known women. Even Margaret Bondfield, an active trade unionist, said she 'deprecated votes for women as the hobby of disappointed old maids whom no one had wanted to marry'. Women 'antis' were very often high achievers who felt that they did not need the vote to be successful. Indeed, their antipathy to the vote led to the formation of an anti-suffrage society of ladies in 1908.

These views were supported by certain groups of men. In 1909 a 'Men's League for Opposing Women's Suffrage' was formed although membership of this group was small, amounting to only 9,000. It used similar tactics to the suffrage groups: groups campaigned across the country, held meetings, collected signatures, and raised funds. In some respects they did rather better than their opponents. During 1908 they collected 337,018 signatures against votes for women whereas the suffragists managed to obtain only 288,736 a year later.

Both suffragists and suffragettes were certainly unsuccessful in persuading many aristocratic and upper-class men to support votes for women. One famous doctor remarked in 1912 that '... there is mixed up with the women's movement much mental disorder'. London's male clubland generally opposed female suffrage as did the Oxford Union. The royal family also opposed female suffrage: Queen Victoria and Edward VII were quite definitely against giving the vote to women.

Despite the lack of success in persuading the government and the majority of the nation to support votes for women there is no doubt that the numbers of women involved in the suffrage movement increased. When women initially campaigned for the vote they drew support from an extremely narrow and exclusive section of society. Even though some historians have argued that the suffrage movement, after 1910, consisted of a rump of Pankurst followers, this is not accurate. By 1914 the female suffrage issue had become the foremost political question and it attracted the support of large numbers of women and many men. Between 1906 and 1914 thousands of women pledged their time, money and energy to the suffrage campaign. After 1907 over 20 new women's suffrage societies were formed, representing a cross-section of professional, religious and political opinion. By 1914 there were 56 societies with a total membership of about 300,000. Working-class and professional women, gymnastic teachers, civil servants and women teachers all had separate groups. The Artists' Suffrage League, Actresses' Franchise League, Women Writers' Suffrage League, Catholic Women's Suffrage Society, Church League for Women's Suffrage, Conservative and Unionist Women's Franchise Association, Free Church League, Friends' League, Jewish League, London Graduates' League, and the Scottish Universities Women's Suffrage Union were amongst the many different suffrage groups. From this list it seemed as if every woman in the country was able to join a suffrage group which represented her profession, religion or interest. There were even organisations for sympathetic men such as the Men's League for

Women's Suffrage and the more militant Men's Political Union which lent support to women's suffrage.

By 1909 the WSPU had 75 office staff who were assisted by hundreds of unpaid volunteers who helped to organise the campaign and publish the newspaper, *Votes for Women*, which had a weekly circulation of 20,000 and a readership that was much larger. Similarly the NUWSS had well over 13,000 members. Funds had also increased dramatically: WSPU funds which had been £1,600 in 1907 jumped to £20,000 by 1914. All of this generated an impressive business enterprise with women successfully marketing and merchandising a whole range of products, from suffragette soap to votes for women porcelain, which publicised the movement and raised even more income.

Active support also increased. In 1908, 1910 and 1911 demonstrations attracted an attendance of 100,000, with the Women's Coronation Procession in June 1911 (to celebrate the crowning of George V) stretching for seven miles. Meetings all over the country were often packed to capacity. Even though opposition groups sometimes collected more signatures on petitions, the suffrage movement's record was still impressive. Petitions were weighed down with signatures. For example in 1902 in Leeds 2,800 out of 3,000 textile workers signed a petition and in 1910 another petition received 300,000 signatures.

There was also a strong international aspect to the women's suffrage movement. In countries with a well-established system of parliamentary democracy women campaigned for the right to vote. An International Women's Suffrage Alliance was founded in 1902. Several States in the USA, most of Australia, New Zealand, and even the Isle of Man had given women the vote. Both the WSPU and the NUWSS had close links with all these countries and it seemed to some as if votes for women was achievable worldwide.

Making notes on *'Women in Political Change'*

In making notes you need to be sure that you capture women's diverse political participation and are aware that women all too often acted in a supportive capacity. Most female activities reinforced stereotypes but occasionally women acted quite violently in pursuit of their goals. The campaigns for women's suffrage are self-explanatory and the subheadings will provide a general framework for your notes.

Answering essay questions on *'Women in Political Change'*

Most essay questions on the suffrage movement concentrate on the reasons why women had not gained the vote by 1914. The following are some examples of this approach.

1. Why had women not won the vote by 1914?
2. How far were women to blame for their failure to win the vote between 1860 and 1914?
3. 'The suffragette movement achieved nothing positive.' Do you agree?
4. How far was suffragette violence responsible for the failure of women to gain the vote?
5. How successful was the suffrage campaign between 1860-1914?

All of these questions require similar content to be used but they also demand a different approach. You will therefore need to switch your material around to suit the wording of the particular question. In each question you need to look at: a) the need for government support; b) the membership, organisation and tactics of the suffrage activists; c) the lack of popular support nationwide. For the twentieth century parts you should also examine: a) the political problems faced by the Liberal party; b) the fact that the suffrage movement was the major political issue for

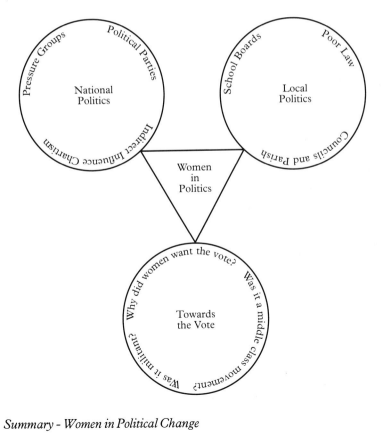

Summary - Women in Political Change

women; c) that peaceful methods had not secured the vote. However, if you choose the questions on the suffragettes, you will need a detailed knowledge of the WSPU and their tactics: for the other questions you must also be aware of change through time - that the political and social situation was quite different in 1860 to 1906.

Source-based questions on '*Women in Political Change*'

1 Women and Education
Read the extract (page 108) on women's work on School Boards. Answer the following questions.
a) How does the source reveal the writer's attitude towards her work on the School Board? (3 marks)
b) To what extent does this attitude affect the value of this as an historical source? (2 marks)
c) What light is thrown by this source on the work of women on School Boards? (5 Marks)

2 Women Councillors
Read the extract (page 106) on the work of women Councillors. Answer the following questions.
a) According to this extract, why were women reluctant to take up council work? (2 marks)
b) What does this source reveal about the values , attitudes and assumptions held by the writer? (4 marks)
c) How useful is this source to a student attempting to acquire an understanding of the work carried out by women in local government? (5 marks)

3 The Polling Booth
Look at the card reproduced on the opposite page, printed and published by the Artists Suffrage League. Answer the following questions.
a) What is meant by 'companions in disgrace'? (1 mark)
b) Why are the two people in the cartoon portrayed in such a way? (2 marks)
c) How effective is this cartoon as propaganda? (3 marks)

4 The Common Cause
Look at the front of the newspaper *The Common Cause* on page 111. Answer the following questions.
a) What comparisons are drawn between pit-brow women, taxation and female suffrage? (3 marks)
b) To what extent does the front page of this paper support the view that the suffrage movement was not middle class? (5 marks)

WSPU propaganda

CHAPTER 7

Conclusion: Changes and Continuities in Women's Lives

On 2 August 1911 a House of Commons Select Committee passed an amendment to a Coal Mines Bill which would prevent women sorting coal on the pit brow. If the Bill became law it would mean the loss of approximately 6,000 female jobs. The case of the pit-brow workers is an interesting one for the historian because it encapsulates some significant changes and continuities in the lives of working-class women during this period.

The 1911 Select Committee, just like the supporters of the 1842 Coal Mines Act, were no less concerned with women's roles as wives and mothers than they were with women's health. Pit-brow work was seen as unsuitable work for women because it allegedly deprived them of their femininity. Much was made of the atmosphere of the pit heads which were covered in coal dust and of the heavy manual labour which made pit-brow work dirty and repulsive and thus 'unsexed' women. Indeed, some of the 1911 Select Committee believed that the pit bank was not a proper place for a woman for 'the proper place for a miner's daughter is at home, at any rate from fourteen to fifteen, to assist the mother in the home; to be educated and trained for their future life as a wife and mother'.

Pit-brow women

As in 1842, much concern was expressed about the health of the miners' children. The Select Committee (influenced by the eugenics movement of the early twentieth century which believed that the British population was becoming less robust) voiced fears that the health of future children might be in jeopardy because of women's work on the pit brow. In addition, it was believed that the consequence of young children being neglected at home when their mothers went out to work was social dislocation. The perceptions of women's role as housewife and mother therefore fuelled the discussion surrounding protective legislation just as it had done in early Victorian England.

Neither the 1911 Select Committee nor the supporters of the 1842 Coal Act believed in women's right to work in the coal industry. On the contrary, the Select Committee, echoing their 1842 counterparts, feared that women unfairly competed for jobs which were the preserve of vulnerable ex-miners: pit-brow work was the refuge of men who were too old or injured to work underground. And because fit and healthy women earned considerably less than their male colleagues it made them an attractively cheap labour force. For example, pit-brow women earned between nine old pence and two shillings a day for work for which men were paid between three shillings and six pence and five shillings a day. If women were 'protected' then employers would have little choice other than to employ the more expensive men.

However the early years of the twentieth century were quite different from those of the early years of the nineteenth century and it is important not to oversimplify attitudes towards women by imagining a seamless continuity. One of the most significant changes between 1842 and 1911 was perhaps the response of women to protective legislation. By 1911, women were unwilling to acquiesce in their 'protection' and, as in an earlier and more famous campaign in 1887, demanded the right to work. Pit-brow women attended and spoke at meetings, went on deputations and wrote petitions to gain public approval for their work. Both the constitutional suffragists and the more militant suffragette organisations gave the pit-brow women ideological and practical support in the campaign to protect their livelihood. For example, the Lancashire and Cheshire Women's Textile and Other Workers Representation Committee argued that it was insulting to women that male MPs voted themselves salaries of £400 a year while voting away the wages of thousands of women. Similarly, the National Union of Women's Suffrage Societies and the Women's Freedom League denounced the amendment as a male conspiracy to stop women's right to work. Perhaps surprisingly, the pit-brow women received most support from the Women's Social and Political Union which, at times, placed their campaigning expertise at the disposal of the pit-brow women. Throughout the campaign *Votes for Women* carried feature articles on the plight of pit-brow women and leading figures such as Annie Kenney organised deputations and meetings to help them. And largely because of this direct political action by both the pit-brow women and the suffrage movement, women, unlike in 1842, won the right to remain working on the pit brow.

By the end of the nineteenth century the world of work for women of both the working and middle class in general had been in many ways turned upside down but like an upturned photograph it was nonetheless recognisable. Working-class women experienced great changes in the type of job they performed both as a result of legislation and because old industries declined and new ones emerged. In some industries, like the cotton trade and the mining industry, women experienced great dislocation as they were compelled to change their working pattern or were else forbidden to work. Other jobs vanished. For example, though few mourned the demise of the gang system, agricultural work for women virtually disappeared as the countryside became mechanised and masculinised. Not surprisingly, given the lack of job opportunities for women, domestic service, though in decline, remained the largest single occupation for women.

Despite changes in the type of work done by working-class women, their work was as much characterised by a sexual division of labour and low pay in the early twentieth century as it had been in the early nineteenth century. In 1914, as in 1815, men and women worked in separate trades. For example, there were certain occupations in which women considerably outnumbered men (e.g. domestic service and dress making) and others in which men far outnumbered women (e.g. engineering and coalmining). Very few women worked in the same occupation as men. One historian has demonstrated that the proportion of all occupations in which women were represented equally with men remained at roughly 25 per cent in the early twentieth century. Even when women worked in the same trade as men they worked in lower grades: women in clerical jobs congregated at the bottom of the employment ladder whereas men held the managerial positions.

The consequences of a sexual division of labour operated against women throughout the whole period because it resulted in skill definitions and pay differentials. Women's work tended to be defined as unskilled whereas men's work was more likely to be defined as skilled: welding was perceived as a skilled job when men did it but when women became welders during the First World War it was reclassified as unskilled with women being paid half the male rate. Women's jobs commanded lower wages whether they were employed on the same job as men or not both in 1815 and 1914. At the outbreak of the First World War, female shopworkers earned about 65 per cent of the male wage, female clerks earned less than a third of the male wage and female typists earned £1 a week whereas men earned £3. Women were also often paid piece rates and found their wage lowered if they earned too much. One factory inspector remarked that 'What can one do when a girl is earning as much as 15 shillings a week but lower the piece rate?' In a survey just before the war the social commentator and reformer, Seebohm Rowntree, had argued that £1 a week was necessary in order to live above poverty but few women received this amount.

Not surprisingly, trades union membership rose dramatically in the period before the First World War. Between 1907 and 1914 women's membership of trade unions rose from 166,803 to 357,956. Given the difficulties faced by women it is remarkable that so many joined trade unions, campaigned for better pay and conditions and participated in strike action. Nonetheless, women's involvement in trade unions remained low. Compared to 30 per cent of men, less than 10 per cent of women workers had joined a union by 1911 which left 90 per cent of women non-unionised. As Mary MacArthur noted in 1914 the 'low standard of living may be stated to be at once the cause and consequence of women's lack of organisation'.

Middle-class women seemed to fare little better than working-class women in the labour market. A few prestigious occupations were beginning to open their doors to women but the majority, such as the legal profession, the stock exchange and the clergy refused them entry. According to the census of 1911 women comprised only 6 per cent of the more prestigious professions such as the Civil Service. Indeed, the 1912 Royal Commission on the Civil Service suggested that they preferred to employ men because they were more able to sustain work, gave continuity of service and were more adaptable to changing circumstances than women. Even when legal obstacles were removed to women's entry to the medical profession they found it extremely difficult to train. Until 1914, when there was a shortage of doctors due to the war, very few hospitals accepted women who wished to become doctors even though women had gained the right to be placed on the Medical Register.

Once accepted into professional occupations, women still did not gain equality. Women formed 75 per cent of elementary school teachers but did not receive the same pay as men nor the same opportunities for promotion. Similarly, women who managed to enter the Civil Service received rates of pay significantly lower than that of men.

Throughout the nineteenth and early twentieth century, women worked hard to improve their lives and the lives of others by means of political activity. At first, women were engaged in a wide range of ventures from Chartism to anti-slavery but by 1914 the campaign for the vote tended to overshadow women's other political involvement.

However, at the outbreak of the First World War it seemed as if women were no further forward in gaining the vote than they had been a hundred years earlier. They had been unsuccessful in persuading the Liberal government to support votes for women, had alienated a vast section of potential allies and had elicited little (male) public support.

However when war broke out the campaign for the vote was abandoned by the major suffrage organisations who led their well-organised party machines to support the war effort. Sylvia Pankhurst's East London Federation of the Suffragettes and Charlotte Despard's Women's Freedom League were in the minority when they criticised the war as an imperialistic one. Yet, despite these setbacks, women had still achieved a great deal: in particular, votes for women was firmly on the political agenda.

Marriage provides the historian with further illustrations of the changes and continuities in women's lives. Whether women were alive in 1815 or 1914 they expected to marry and have children as this young woman recalled in 1914: 'she could never remember a time when she had not known that a woman's failure or success in life depended entirely on whether or not she succeeded in getting a husband. It was not even a question of marrying well...any husband at all was better than none.' For the majority of women marriage remained an economic necessity in 1914 as it had been in 1815.

Nevertheless, the nature of the marriage contract had changed considerably. Legal reform had ensured that women were no longer considered to be the goods and chattels of their husbands but enjoyed almost equal legal status with men in marriage. Women could no longer be locked up and beaten, they were able to own and dispose of their property within marriage, keep their earnings from their work and make contracts with other people. However, although the virtual slavery of marriage in 1815 had at last been eroded by the fundamental revisions in property law, legal equality had still not been achieved: for example, men continued to have the right to rape their wives in marriage.

If the society heiress Caroline Norton had been alive in 1914 she might have been surprised by quite dramatic changes in the infant custody law as women, not men, were granted guardianship of children after a couple had separated. Indeed, in 1910 legal history was made when an adulterous and divorced woman was given custody of a child from a previous marriage because the court believed that 'the benefit and interest of the infant is the paramount consideration, and not the punishment of the guilty party'. This court decision may have been a dramatic reversal of previous practice but it reinforced women's role as wife and mother and absolved fathers of a degree of responsibility towards their children.

At least one historian has suggested that the most important change in married women's lives was the decline in family size. At the beginning of the nineteenth century, women's lives were monopolised by constant childbirth as married women on average produced between five and six children, over 40 per cent of married women had more than seven children and a particularly fertile 16 per cent had more than ten children. By 1914, largely because of the popularity of birth control, the size of the average family had dropped to under three allowing many women to be physically freed from the yearly round of pregnancy. Even so, the advocates and practitioners of birth control were predominantly middle class. A book entitled *Maternity* which was published during the war contained letters from working-class women regretting the lack of contraceptive advice available to them. Consequently, perhaps because of the absence of effective birth control provision, working-class family size remained higher than that of the middle and upper class.

Educational change was quite contradictory. At the beginning of the nineteenth century, except for a small elite, education for all classes of girls and young women was virtually non-existent. By 1914 the educational revolution for girls appeared more or less complete. Board Schools provided education for working-class girls whereas private and public schools catered for the middle class. Higher education for women was also provided as more and more universities opened their previously closed doors to women. However, this perceived progress must be viewed with care as the educational opportunities for girls and women were still set within a gendered and class framework which at times consolidated, rather than challenged, women's role as wife and mother.

Working-class girls appeared to have benefited from state intervention in education as, for the first time in British history, education was both free and compulsory. However, working-class girls, to a large extent, were taught subjects which confirmed both their class and their gender roles. Cooking and laundry lessons dominated the curriculum of Board Schools and was backed up by text books which extolled the virtues of domestic service as the following manual printed in 1894 suggests: 'Teachers should, when possible, advise mothers to encourage their daughters to become good domestic servants in preference to entering upon different callings which frequently entail late hours, injury to health and exposure to temptation.' To a cynical eye, state education seemed to compound class and gender stereotypes by preparing working-class girls for low-paid, working-class and female occupations.

The free state system of education was rarely utilised by middle-class parents who sent their daughters to feepaying schools, the most prestigious of which offered a broad curriculum. Unfortunately, the objectives of most girls' schools remained non-intellectual ones as large numbers of them merely aimed to teach young women basic accomplishments. However, it must be remembered that the vast majority of middle-class girls in 1914 did not attend school but were taught at home by their mothers, governesses or tutors as their grandmothers had been before them.

Despite the efforts of reformers and the intervention of government, prostitution continued largely because the underlying causes of prostitution had not been addressed. By 1914 the managers of penitentiaries and asylums finally realised that it was too difficult a task to reform an individual prostitute and so immediately after the First World War, many of these institutions became homes for single mothers. However, social purity groups continued their fight against prostitution. For example, in 1912 a campaign was waged to pass a

Criminal Law Amendment Act (CLAA) to halt the perceived increase of white slavery. This Act permitted the arrest of those suspected of procuring young girls and required landlords to evict known prostitutes. Although the social climate of the Edwardian period was quite distinct from the Victorian era there were great similarities between those who supported the 1912 CLAA and those who had given support to the 1885 Act. In a series of articles, published in the *Suffragette* in 1913, Christabel Pankhurst - just as feminists had before her - criticised the double standard of morality, blamed men for the increase of venereal disease and proclaimed 'Votes for women and chastity for men'. Yet, by 1914 social purity groups, as in the 1880s, were still in the minority as not even the combined strength of all the various associations was able to convince the nation of the need for such moral scrutiny.

In 1914, therefore, a young woman of 17 who looked back at her great grandmothers' life in 1815 would notice considerable changes between their two circumstances. This same young girl might also be gladdened that her prospective future offered greater opportunities than that of her relative. However it is important not to adopt what historians call a teleological approach (an approach, as in Whig or Marxist history, whereby history was seen to have a goal or purpose) to women's history. If this approach is used uncritically it is easy to assume that women were predestined to reach the goal of emancipation by the twentieth century. Indeed, the concept of progress presupposes assumptions about an ideal state of affairs to which women could aspire. Fortunately, the idea of an unbroken straight line of progress has been abandoned by historians who now view history as a series of uneven developments. Change, as demonstrated in this book, does not always mean improvement.

In addition, the changes in the role of women cannot usefully be analysed outside a political, economic and social context. It is fair to assume that the majority of lives of most people had improved by 1914 in comparison with lives in 1815. The standard of living had risen, life expectancy had improved, there was better health care, sanitary reforms and better pay and hours of work. Women, who made up more than 50 per cent of the British population, obviously shared in these achievements. Nevertheless the examination of particular areas of women's lives has shown that the changes and improvements were contradictory.

This book has examined a number of key issues and has attempted to provide an overview of some of the significant changes in women's lives between 1814 and 1914. It has been divided into separate sections each of which has examined one important aspect such as marriage, education, work, politics and morality. However, it is important to stress that women's lives in reality were not divided in such discrete compartments. Changes which occurred in one part of their lives influenced and were influenced by other factors. For example, the increased use of birth control which led to smaller families gave women a little more personal space which in turn facilitated their political involvement. In contrast, women's role in the family, combined with limited educational opportunities, confirmed women's role in the labour market.

By 1914, women had achieved some degree of marital equality, had been given some educational opportunities and had begun to make some inroads into traditionally male occupations. They had attempted to impose a moral order and had focussed political action on winning the vote. Nevertheless, equality with men was a long way off and you might like to consider whether there was more change in the period covered by this book or in the years since 1914.

Working on 'Conclusion: Changes and Continuities in Women's Lives'

You need to have a view on the extent to which women were emancipated by 1914. You may adopt an optimistic approach whereby you view the period between 1815 and 1914 as one of gradual improvement in all its varied aspects. On the other hand, you may favour a radical feminist perspective and decide that in a 100-year period women's lives had not advanced that significantly because men remained all powerful. You may, however, prefer to weigh up the benefits accrued by women in this period against the disadvantages which remained. Whatever your chosen opinion, you need to justify it. To do this, you will need to refer back to your notes and earlier chapters in order to build up an argument based on fact rather than opinion.

This is not an easy task so needs to be done at the end, rather than at the beginning, of your studies. It involves some hard thinking rather than regurgitation of the facts. And as Keith Randell, the editor of this series, states 'if the prospect daunts you somewhat, it is worth remembering that for most people thinking about issues is much harder than learning the facts... but the effort involved in acquiring the skill is normally repaid many times over during the average person's life!'.

Chronological Table

1792   Mary Wollstonecraft's Vindication of the Rights of Women

1798   First Magdalen Home opened in London

1803   Abortion Act: death penalty for attempted abortion by drugs

1807   London Female Penitentiary founded

1819   Peterloo

1828   Abortion Act: death penalty for attempted abortion by instruments
Birmingham Female Society for the Relief of British Negro Slaves founded

1832   'Great' Reform Act

1834   Poor Law Amendment Act

1837   Civil Marriage introduced: Roman Catholics and Nonconformists allowed own ceremonies
Death penalty for abortion abolished

1838   Beginnings of Chartism

1839   Infant Custody Act: mothers given custody of children under the age of 7 and access to their children up to 16
Rebecca riots and Anti-Poor Law riots begin

1841   Women involved in Anti-Corn Law League

1842   Plug riots
Mines and Collieries Act prohibited women from working underground

1843   Governesses Benevolent Institution founded

1844   Factory Act limited hours of work for female textile workers

1847   Ten Hours Act

1848   Queens College founded

1849   Bedford College founded

1851   Church Penitentiary Association founded

1857   Divorce and Matrimonial Causes Act

1858   Dorothea Beale became Principal of Cheltenham Ladies' College

1859   Elizabeth Blackwell's name placed on British Medical Register
Association for Promoting the Employment of Women founded

1860   School of Nursing founded at St Thomas's hospital, London by Florence Nightingale
Medical profession denied medical registration to those who held foreign degrees

1861   Abortion Act
Age of sexual consent fixed at 12

1862   Female Emigration Society founded

1863   Girls allowed to take local examinations for Cambridge and Oxford

1864   First Contagious Diseases Act passed

1865   Women's Suffrage Society founded in Manchester

1866   WSS became National Women's Suffrage Society
Women's Suffrage Petition

1867   Second Reform Act
J.S. Mill and Harriet Taylor's *On the Subjection of Women* published
North of England Council for the Higher Education of Women founded
Royal Commission on Employment of Children, Young Persons and Women in Agriculture

1869   Unmarried ratepaying women given vote on municipal councils
Women admitted to Owens College, Manchester
Ladies National Association founded

1870   Married Women's Property Act
Women eligible to vote on School Boards

1871   Girls Public Day School Company founded

1872   Secret ballot in parliamentary elections
Women employed in Post Office Savings Bank

1873   Infants Custody Act
Girton College, Cambridge founded
Social Purity Alliance founded

1874   Jane Nassau appointed to workhouse inspectorate

1875   First woman Poor Law Guardian elected
Women clerks employed at National Savings Bank
Age of sexual consent raised to 13

1876   Women clerks employed at Post Office

1877   Start of Besant/Bradlaugh trial

1878   Matrimonial Causes Act: Courts given power to give a separation order with maintenance to a woman whose husband had been convicted of assault
London University admitted women
Maria Grey Teachers' Training College opened
Domestic economy established as a compulsory subject in Board Schools

1880   Industrial Schools Act allowed local authorities to remove children thought to be in moral danger from parents

1881 New Civil Service grade of women clerk introduced
House of Lords Commission on the Protection of Young Girls

1882 Women journalists employed by W.H. Stead
Married Women's Property Act gave women control of the
money she brought to marriage and acquired after it
Grants given to schools for teaching cookery

1883 White Cross Army and Church of England Purity Society
founded
Royal Holloway College, London, founded

1884 Women admitted to Primrose League
Third Reform Act

1885 Criminal Law Amendment Act raised age of consent to 16 and
made male homosexuality illegal
National Vigilance Society founded

1886 Maintenance of Wives (Desertion) Act gave magistrates power
to grant maintenance
Women's Liberal Federation founded
Custody of Infants Act
Contagious Diseases Act repealed

1887 Royal British Nurses Association founded
Attempts to exclude women from the pit brow failed

1888 First woman elected to London County Council

1890 Grants given to schools for teaching laundry

1891 Regina v. Jackson case. Husbands no longer able to abduct
separated wives

1893 Independent Labour Party formed in Bradford
First woman factory inspector appointed

1894 Women allowed to participate in parish, district and church
councils
Property qualifications abolished for Poor Law Guardians

1895 Summary Jurisdiction Act: established grounds by which
battered women could obtain a divorce

1897 National Union of Women's Suffrage Society founded

1903 Women's Social and Political Union founded

1906 Liberals win landslide election

1907 Women admitted to all aspects of local government
First WSPU paper printed
Women's Freedom League formed as breakaway group from the
WSPU by Charlotte Despard

1908 Asquith Prime Minister
First window smashers and hunger strike

1910   Year of truce by militant suffragettes
       Conciliation Bill which promised vote to propertied women lost
       Black Friday of suffragettes
       Women allowed to take Chartered Accountants exam
1911   Second Conciliation Bill shelved after second reading
       East London Federation of Suffragettes founded by Sylvia
       Pankhurst
1912   Third Conciliation Bill failed second reading
       Pethwick Lawrences left WSPU
       Christabel Pankhurst fled to Paris, France
1913   Prisoners Temporary Discharge Bill
       Death of Emily Wilding Davidson
       Private members bill for votes for women defeated
1914   ELFS splits from the WSPU
       First World War began
       WSPU joined war effort but ELFS and WFL did not
1918   Sex Disqualification Removal Act
1919   Legal profession opened to women
1922   First woman barrister
1928   Women over the age of 21 obtain the vote

Acknowledgements

The publishers would like to thank the following for permission to reproduce material in this volume:

Sidgwick and Jackson for the illustration of Dr Patterson's Pills from *A Secret World of Sex*, Steve Humphries, (1988); Historical Association for extracts from 'Women in an Industrializing Society: England 1750-1880', *Historical Associaiton Studies* 1990, Jane Rendall; Penguin for extracts from *Strong Minded Women,* Janet Horowitz Murray; Basil Blackwell for extracts from *Unequal Opportunities,* Angela John and *Equal or Different,* Jane Rendall (ed); The Clarendon Press for extracts from *Ladies Elect,* Patricia Hollis; Cambridge University Press for extracts from *Prostitution and Victorian Society,* J Walkowitz.

Further Reading

There are a number of general books on women's history but no one book exists which provides an overview of all the aspects covered in this book. Women's history is still characterised by specialist texts which examine various aspects of women's history. Nonetheless there are a few books which provide a good introduction to the period such as **Tilly and Scott's** *Women, Work and Family* (Methuen, 1987) which discusses the relationships between women's role as housewife and mother and her role in the workplace. Similarly, **Catherine Hall's** *White, Male and Middle Class* (Polity, 1992) and **Leonore Davidoff's** *Worlds Between, Historical Perspectives on Gender and Class* (Polity, 1995) both offer essays on a wide variety of women's history which are useful for students. **June Purvis's** *Women's History,* (UCL, 1995) published just as this book goes to press, also provides an excellent survey of women's history for undergraduate students.

There are a number of books which look at women's role in the family but most are characterised by an empirical rather than an analytical or theoretical approach. **Joan Perkin's** *Women and Marriage in Nineteenth Century England* (Routledge, 1989) is characteristic of the 'women's history' type of approach but provides an extremely readable introduction to the topic of marriage, whilst the social historian **Laurence Stone's** highly readable *Broken Lives* sums up the situation of divorce. For students with a legal interest **Mary Lyndon Shanley's** scholarly and detailed *Feminism, Marriage and the Law in Victorian England* (Princeton Paperbacks, 1989) is an admirable study of the changes in the legal system of England. **Angus McLaren's** *Birth Control in Nineteenth Century England* (Holmes and Meier 1978) demonstrates that the decline of the birth rate in late Victorian England was one of the most important social changes to occur. By far the best book on Queen Victoria has to be **Dorothy Thompson's** *Queen Victoria* (Virago, 1990) which offers an exciting interpretive overview of Victoria's life from a gendered perspective.

There is a limited historiography on women's education in the nineteenth century and tends to be dominated by the feminist historian **June Purvis.** The best introduction is her *A History of Women's Education in England* (Open University, 1991) which examines the education of working-class and middle-class girls and women. In this very enjoyable book Purvis argues, convincingly, that a middle-class ideology of femininity shaped education for all girls, regardless of class. An alternative interpretation is found in **Felicity Hunt's** *Lessons for Life,* (Basil Blackwell, 1987) which is a collection of essays by different historians and explores in various ways how education, at one and the same time, both reflected and reinforced gender divisions.

Women's work has the longest and largest historiographical tradition.

The best short introductions to this topic are **Elizabeth Roberts'** *Women's Work, 1840-1940* (Macmillan, 1988) which outlines the work of working-class women and the responses of the women and the government to it and **Jane Rendall's** *Women in an Industrializing Society: England 1750-1880* (Historical Association, 1990) which draws upon recent work to analyse the role of women both at work and in the family. Specialist texts such as **Angela V. John's** *By the Sweat of Their Brow* (Routledge, 1984) provide excellent and highly readable analyses of coalmining women in the nineteenth century. Students with a sociological interest might like to read **Sonya Rose's** intellectually challenging *Limited Livelihoods*, (Routledge, 1992) which argues that gender was a central organising principle of working life in the nineteenth century.

Prostitution has only recently captured the attention of feminist historians. Two books which broke new ground are **Judith Walkowitz's** *Prostitution and Victorian Society*, (Cambridge, 1980) and **Linda Mahood's** *The Magdalenes*. (Routledge, 1990). Both are written from a loosely defined socialist feminist perspective which has been influenced by the debate on gender and by the work of the post-structuralists. Their topics are different as Walkowitz examines the Contagious Diseases Acts whereas Mahood looks at reform institutions in Scotland.

The political participation of women, other than the suffrage movement, has not been written in any great depth. **Jane Rendall's** *Equal or Different* (Basil Blackwell, 1987) is a wide-ranging collection of essays which examines women's varied role in politics. **Clare Midgley's** *Women against Slavery* (Routledge, 1992) provides an in-depth analysis of women who participated in one particular pressure group while **Malcolm Thomis** and **Jennifer Grimmett's** *Women in Protest, 1800-1850* (Croom Helm, 1982) is a much-needed descriptive examination of women involved in a variety of *ad hoc* groups and organisations. One of the most recent texts on women's political involvement is **Anna Clark's,** *The Struggle for the Breeches: Gender and the Making of the British Working Class* (Rivers Oram Press, 1995) which is important for an understanding of radical politics. The suffrage movement has been written about at length but one of the crucial texts which broke the Pankhurst myth has to be **Liddington** and **Norris's** *One Hand Tied Behind Us* (Virago, 1978) which examines the role played by working-class women in the fight for the vote.

Index